Revocable Trusts: A Complete Guide to Estate Planning and Asset Protection

PUBLISHED BY Bryce Caldwell

Table of contents

Introduction

Estate planning has always existed as a practice bound up with the universal human desire to provide continuity, stability, and security for those we leave behind. Yet the modern world has altered the scale, complexity, and urgency of these concerns in ways that earlier generations could scarcely have imagined. Today, families live longer lives, often across multiple jurisdictions, while simultaneously holding assets that may be physical, financial, or digital in nature. Wealth is no longer confined to a home, a parcel of land, or a savings account. It can be represented in securities, intellectual property, cryptocurrency, online businesses, or even carefully curated social media brands. These changes have created a pressing need to rethink how we approach estate planning in the twenty-first century. The traditional reliance on a simple will, or the assumption that assets would naturally flow to heirs with minimal friction, has given way to the recognition that without deliberate preparation, much of what one has built can be squandered in lengthy probate proceedings, excessive taxation, or family disputes.

To understand the modern need for estate planning, one must first appreciate the shifting cultural and economic context. Families are more fragmented, with many individuals experiencing second or third marriages, stepchildren, or long-term partnerships without formal marriage. Geographic mobility means that heirs may be spread across continents. The rise of blended families, cross-border inheritances, and diverse asset classes introduces a level of complexity that makes a casual or improvised approach deeply risky. Moreover, as healthcare advances extend life expectancy, more people are living with diminished capacity in later years, requiring plans that not only govern the distribution of assets after death but also provide for decision-making during life. Questions of guardianship, medical directives, and powers of attorney are inseparable from the larger project of safeguarding a lifetime's work.

At the same time, the legal and financial frameworks that regulate inheritance have become more intricate. Tax codes shift with political winds, probate courts are often overburdened, and the costs of litigation can easily erode estates that are not properly protected. What once could be settled in a family meeting now frequently requires careful navigation of statutory requirements, institutional bureaucracy, and judicial oversight. In this environment, the absence of an estate plan is not merely an oversight—it is a costly liability. It exposes loved ones to confusion and conflict, while giving courts and creditors greater authority than the deceased would ever have intended.

Against this backdrop, the revocable trust has emerged as one of the most powerful tools in contemporary estate planning. Unlike static instruments that speak only after death, a revocable trust is designed to be dynamic, adaptable, and administratively efficient. It allows an individual—the grantor—to retain control of assets during life, while providing a seamless mechanism for their transfer upon incapacity or death. At its core, the trust separates ownership from control, placing assets under the stewardship of a trustee who acts for the benefit of named beneficiaries. This structure achieves several critical goals at once: it bypasses probate, it preserves privacy, it ensures continuity of asset management, and it allows for tailored distribution in accordance with the grantor's wishes.

The essential feature of revocability gives this tool its modern appeal. Because the grantor can amend or revoke the trust at any time during life, it provides flexibility that acknowledges the realities of change. Families evolve, fortunes fluctuate, and priorities shift. A rigid plan is often a poor plan, but a revocable trust accommodates these transitions without sacrificing structure. Whether someone acquires new property, undergoes a major life event such as divorce or remarriage, or simply rethinks how they wish to distribute their estate, the revocable trust allows for modification with relative ease.

Another reason these trusts have become indispensable lies in their capacity to shield heirs from avoidable burdens. Probate is not only time-consuming—often stretching from months into years—but also public and costly. In many jurisdictions, the fees associated with probate consume a significant percentage of the estate, effectively diminishing the inheritance left to beneficiaries. By transferring assets into a revocable trust, one circumvents this process, ensuring that successors gain access more swiftly and with less expense. Privacy is equally crucial in an era when public court records can expose family wealth to unwanted scrutiny or opportunistic claims. A trust administers these transfers quietly, outside the glare of the courtroom.

Equally significant is the role of the revocable trust in planning for incapacity. While wills only speak at death, a trust functions immediately upon the grantor's inability to manage their affairs. This continuity is especially important as life expectancy rises and conditions such as dementia become more prevalent. Without such provisions, families are often forced into guardianship proceedings to determine who may act on behalf of an incapacitated individual—a process that can be emotionally and financially draining. A revocable trust, by contrast, names a successor trustee in advance, eliminating uncertainty and preserving the dignity of the grantor's intentions.

This guide has been created to illuminate how estate planning, and revocable trusts in particular, can serve as cornerstones of asset protection in our time. Its purpose is not to overwhelm with legal jargon, nor to present estate planning as a task reserved for the wealthy. Rather, it aims to demonstrate that careful planning is relevant to anyone who has worked to build a life, regardless of the size of their estate. The principles discussed here apply equally to a family with a modest home and retirement account as they do to an entrepreneur with diverse global holdings. What matters is not the scale but the foresight.

Throughout these pages, you will find a careful balance of explanation and application. The aim is not only to describe what revocable trusts are, but also to situate them within the broader logic of estate planning. You will see how they interact with wills, powers of attorney, and advance healthcare directives. You will discover how they can be structured to address the particular challenges of blended families, special needs dependents, or business succession. You will also gain a sense of the broader ethical and psychological dimensions of estate planning—the peace of mind that comes from knowing that one's affairs are in order, the relief that comes from sparing loved ones unnecessary disputes, and the empowerment that comes from making deliberate choices about one's legacy.

In exploring these subjects, this guide acknowledges that estate planning is not merely a technical exercise. It is a deeply human endeavor that speaks to values, relationships, and aspirations. To create a trust is to articulate what one wishes to endure beyond their lifetime. It is an act of stewardship that affirms responsibility not only for material possessions but also for the well-being of those who will receive them. The decisions made in these pages are therefore never abstract; they are intimately tied to the lives of children, spouses, parents, and communities.

Ultimately, this book seeks to transform your approach to asset protection by reframing it as a proactive and empowering process. Too often, estate planning is delayed or dismissed because it is associated with morbidity or complexity. But when understood correctly, it becomes a tool of clarity and compassion. It frees you from uncertainty and equips those you love with guidance instead of burdens. By demystifying revocable trusts and situating them within the larger framework of modern estate planning, this guide enables you to take control of your financial narrative, preserve your intentions, and leave behind not confusion but coherence.

The chapters that follow will delve into the historical roots of trusts, their evolution in law, their adaptability in the digital age, and their practical applications across diverse family and financial contexts. Along the way, you will be provided with insights, examples, and explanations that reveal both the technical precision and the human significance of these instruments. By the end, you will not only understand the mechanics of estate planning but also appreciate its power to protect, preserve, and pass on the fruits of a lifetime's labor.

In this spirit, consider the pages ahead not as a sterile legal manual, but as a map. It is a map to security, continuity, and peace of mind. It is an invitation to take deliberate steps today that will shape how your legacy is remembered tomorrow. The need is modern, the tools are essential, and the opportunity is yours to embrace.

Chapter 1: The Evolution of Trust Law and Modern Applications

"The best time to plant a tree was 20 years ago. The second best time is now." — Chinese Proverb

It is often said that estate planning is about foresight, and nowhere is this more evident than in the history of trusts. For centuries, the trust has functioned as a legal and practical instrument to safeguard wealth, manage property, and secure the continuity of families and institutions. A telling statistic underscores the urgency of understanding this instrument in the modern era: more than 68% of Americans die without a will, leaving their estates exposed to costly probate proceedings, which can reduce estate value by 3–7% or more. The trust, particularly the revocable trust, has emerged as a solution that minimizes such losses and ensures that a lifetime of work is preserved for those it was intended to benefit. To appreciate the power of trusts today, however, one must begin with their origins, trace their evolution, and recognize how they have been adapted to fit both American law and the digital realities of the twenty-first century.

1.1 Historical Foundation of Trust Structures

Origins in English Common Law and the Crusades

The earliest recognizable form of the trust traces back to medieval England, during a time when societal structures were rigid and property ownership was closely tied to feudal obligations. Under English common law, landownership was not only a matter of wealth but also of loyalty to the Crown and feudal lords. The rigid legal framework of the time made it difficult for individuals to transfer or manage property in ways that accounted for absence, incapacity, or strategic succession.

The Crusades of the twelfth and thirteenth centuries played a pivotal role in the emergence of what we now identify as trust structures. Knights and landowners who departed on extended campaigns to the Holy Land faced a pressing dilemma: how could they ensure their estates would be managed and preserved during their long absences, often lasting years, while still ensuring their families would retain the benefits of their holdings? Many of these men conveyed legal title of their land to trusted friends or relatives, instructing them to manage the property for the benefit of their families while they were away.

What developed from this practice was the concept of "uses," which later evolved into the legal doctrine of *cestui que use*. The knight or landowner would give nominal ownership to a trustee, with the expectation—moral at first, and then legal—that the trustee would manage the land faithfully and return it upon demand or pass the benefits to designated heirs. This separation of legal ownership from equitable benefit became the foundation of trust law. Although disputes were inevitable, courts of equity stepped in to enforce these arrangements, recognizing the rights of beneficiaries even when common law failed to acknowledge them. This intervention established a dual system: the trustee held title under common law, while the beneficiary's rights were protected by equity.

The importance of this development cannot be overstated. By separating legal and beneficial ownership, the trust introduced a flexible framework that could adapt to changing needs. It was not merely a workaround for absent knights; it became a durable mechanism for managing property beyond the strict confines of feudal law. Over time, the "use" evolved into the modern trust, with clearly defined roles for settlors (or grantors), trustees, and beneficiaries.

Evolution from Wartime Necessities to Legal Innovation

The medieval roots of trusts reveal how necessity drives innovation. The unpredictability of war, the danger of death in battle, and the uncertainties of return forced families to think creatively about continuity. These wartime necessities shaped the development of estate planning tools, embedding within them a principle of resilience. Trusts were not designed only for wealth but for survival and continuity, ensuring that dependents were not left destitute when their protector was absent or deceased.

As the centuries progressed, the structure of trusts became increasingly formalized. English Chancery Courts, operating on principles of fairness and equity, recognized the enforceability of these arrangements. They established the idea that trustees owed fiduciary duties—duties of loyalty, prudence, and impartiality—to the beneficiaries. This doctrine would eventually influence modern notions of fiduciary responsibility, extending far beyond trusts into corporate law and financial management.

By the early modern period, trusts had become versatile instruments. They were used to preserve family estates across generations, avoid the Crown's taxes and restrictions, and ensure that property was managed according to the wishes of its original owner. What began as a wartime solution had blossomed into a sophisticated legal tool, adaptable to both personal and financial needs.

American Adaptation and State Law Variations

When the trust crossed the Atlantic with English settlers, it carried with it centuries of legal development. Colonial America adopted the trust as part of its legal inheritance from English common law, but soon modified it to meet the unique conditions of a new society. Land in the colonies was abundant compared to England, but its distribution and management required mechanisms that could adapt to different family structures, economic pursuits, and legal traditions.

In the United States, trust law became a matter largely governed by state statutes and judicial decisions, which meant that variations quickly emerged. One key distinction that continues to this day lies in the contrast between community property states and common law states. In community property jurisdictions, typically influenced by Spanish and French traditions, property acquired during marriage is considered jointly owned by both spouses, regardless of who holds the title. In common law states, ownership is determined by title and contribution, leading to different estate planning strategies. These distinctions affect how trusts are drafted, how marital property is treated within them, and how assets are distributed upon death or divorce.

As American society grew more complex, the need for greater uniformity became evident. To address inconsistencies across jurisdictions, the Uniform Trust Code (UTC) was introduced in the early twenty-first century. The UTC sought to provide a model framework that states could adopt or adapt, offering consistency in trust creation, administration, and enforcement. While not all states have adopted the UTC in its entirety, its influence has been profound, offering a shared language and set of standards that modernized trust law in the United States.

Through this codification, trusts became more accessible to ordinary people, not just the wealthy elite. They provided clarity about fiduciary duties, expanded the rights of beneficiaries, and standardized processes such as modification or termination of trusts. By reducing uncertainty, the UTC enhanced public confidence in trusts as reliable tools of estate planning.

Digital Age Transformations in Trust Management

The evolution of trusts did not halt with the adoption of the UTC. The twenty-first century has introduced entirely new challenges and opportunities that trust law has had to address. The digital revolution, globalization of assets, and the rise of intangible property have forced estate planning to expand beyond traditional boundaries.

Electronic signature laws and remote notarization have dramatically altered the practical administration of trusts. Where once every amendment or notarized document required physical presence, digital tools now allow for remote execution, bringing efficiency and accessibility to the process. This development proved particularly valuable during global disruptions such as the COVID-19 pandemic, when travel and in-person meetings were restricted. Today, many jurisdictions accept electronically signed trust documents as legally binding, provided certain safeguards are observed.

Equally transformative has been the inclusion of digital assets in estate planning. Cryptocurrencies, online businesses, intellectual property in digital form, and even collections of digital art require careful integration into trusts. Unlike physical property, digital assets are often protected by passwords, encryption, and third-party custodianship. Without proper planning, such assets can be lost forever. Trust structures now often include provisions for managing and transferring these digital properties, ensuring continuity of access and preservation of value.

Artificial intelligence and automation are also beginning to play a role in trust administration. Some platforms now offer AI-assisted monitoring of trust distributions, ensuring compliance with the grantor's instructions and alerting trustees to anomalies. Automated mechanisms can release funds upon certain conditions being met, such as the beneficiary reaching a certain age, completing educational milestones, or triggering health-related provisions. While these tools cannot replace the human judgment required of trustees, they augment efficiency and reduce the risk of oversight.

In this way, the trust—once a solution for medieval knights embarking on perilous journeys—has become a modern instrument capable of managing assets that exist entirely in cyberspace. The principles remain the same: separating control from benefit, protecting the vulnerable, and ensuring continuity. Yet the applications reflect a world that is vastly more interconnected, digital, and dynamic than the one that gave birth to the concept.

1.2 Contemporary Trust Applications Beyond Traditional Estate Planning

Although the trust was originally conceived as a mechanism for protecting landholdings and ensuring that heirs could enjoy the fruits of their inheritance without interruption, it has expanded far beyond those traditional roots. Today, revocable and irrevocable trusts have become central to financial planning strategies that touch nearly every corner of modern life, from running a business to managing international assets to securing the future of vulnerable family members. This expansion reflects the adaptability of the trust structure and its ability to evolve in response to economic, social, and technological pressures.

One of the most significant applications of trusts outside conventional estate distribution lies in business succession planning. For family-owned enterprises, the question of continuity is both practical and emotional. A business represents not only financial value but also the history, reputation, and collective labor of multiple generations. Without careful planning, the sudden incapacity or death of a principal owner can cause instability, jeopardizing employees, clients, and family alike. Revocable trusts can be structured to hold business interests, ensuring that ownership transitions occur smoothly when triggered by specific events. When integrated with buy-sell agreements, they establish a framework where surviving owners or designated heirs can assume control with minimal disruption. This coordination often pairs with key person insurance policies, which provide liquidity in the event of the loss of a central figure, making sure that the enterprise remains solvent during periods of uncertainty. Beyond continuity, such arrangements also enable tax efficiency, reducing exposure to estate or capital gains taxes and ensuring that the enterprise is not dismantled to satisfy unforeseen liabilities. In this way, the trust becomes both a safety net and a strategic tool for sustaining economic vitality across generations.

Trusts have also become indispensable in the realm of international asset management. The globalization of wealth means that families may own property in multiple countries, maintain bank accounts abroad, or invest in foreign companies. These cross-border holdings complicate estate planning, as each jurisdiction applies its own rules to taxation, reporting, and inheritance. To address this complexity, specialized trusts are designed to comply with foreign grantor trust rules, ensuring that the settlor is not unintentionally exposed to double taxation or onerous penalties. Pre-immigration planning is another critical dimension. High-net-worth individuals relocating to the United States, for example, often establish trusts prior to arrival in order to shield existing wealth from certain U.S. tax regimes. These structures can lock in favorable treatment while still providing beneficiaries with access to income or distributions as needed. Compliance has become even more pressing with international agreements such as the Foreign Account Tax Compliance Act (FATCA) and various bilateral tax treaties. Trusts serve as vehicles for consolidating reporting obligations, preserving transparency, and avoiding the severe consequences of noncompliance. By managing foreign holdings through carefully crafted trusts, individuals and families not only protect their assets but also create a coherent strategy for global wealth stewardship.

Another arena where contemporary trust applications shine is in special needs and multi-generational planning. Families with dependents who have disabilities face unique challenges, as government benefit programs are often means-tested. A direct inheritance can disqualify a beneficiary from receiving critical medical or financial support. Special needs trusts resolve this dilemma by holding assets in a way that supplements, rather than replaces, public assistance. Trustees are empowered to provide for extra needs—such as therapies, educational opportunities, or personal enrichment—without jeopardizing eligibility for benefits. At the same time, these trusts preserve dignity by allowing loved ones to maintain quality of life without unnecessary sacrifice.

Multi-generational planning is equally transformative. Families increasingly recognize that wealth should not only transfer from parent to child but also extend to grandchildren and beyond. Educational funding is a natural focus here, but traditional approaches can unintentionally hinder eligibility for financial aid. Trusts can be designed to provide tuition support while avoiding negative impacts on aid calculations, striking a balance between generosity and prudence. More broadly, legacy trusts or dynasty trusts allow wealth to be preserved for multiple generations, insulating assets from creditors, divorces, or market volatility. Importantly, these instruments can adapt to changing family circumstances, ensuring that resources remain available while respecting evolving priorities. Whether it is supporting entrepreneurship in one generation or medical needs in another, the trust becomes a living framework that reflects both stability and flexibility.

The unifying theme across these contemporary applications is that trusts have outgrown the limited function of death-time transfers. They now operate as dynamic vehicles for business resilience, international compliance, and familial continuity, integrating seamlessly with broader financial strategies. By accommodating modern realities, they offer solutions that neither wills nor informal arrangements can match.

1.3 Integration with Modern Financial Instruments

The twenty-first century has also witnessed a profound integration of trusts with cutting-edge financial instruments and technologies. This fusion has transformed not only the administration of trusts but also the kinds of assets they hold and the ways they deliver value to beneficiaries. Far from being static legal devices, modern trusts now operate at the intersection of finance, technology, and risk management.

Technology-enhanced trust administration is perhaps the most visible sign of this evolution. Blockchain technology, initially developed to power cryptocurrencies, has been adapted for secure documentation and verification in trust law. By recording trust agreements, amendments, and transactions on immutable ledgers, blockchain systems provide transparency and prevent tampering, reducing the potential for fraud or mismanagement. In parallel, digital vaults allow critical documents—such as powers of attorney, healthcare directives, and succession instructions—to be securely stored and accessed by authorized parties worldwide. These vaults ensure that trustees and beneficiaries can retrieve vital information instantly, regardless of location, minimizing delays that historically plagued estate administration. The rise of robo-advisors adds another dimension, enabling algorithm-driven investment strategies to be integrated into trust portfolios. Trustees can leverage these platforms for low-cost, diversified management while maintaining oversight, thereby combining technological efficiency with fiduciary accountability.

Trusts are also increasingly being used to channel investments into alternative asset classes, reflecting the broader diversification strategies of sophisticated investors. Real estate investment trusts (REITs) offer exposure to property markets without the administrative burdens of direct ownership, while some trusts still hold tangible real estate to anchor family wealth in physical assets. Beyond property, trusts can invest in private equity, venture capital, and hedge funds, gaining access to high-growth opportunities typically reserved for institutional investors. These vehicles can provide significant returns but also carry heightened risk, which makes the protective structure of a trust especially valuable. Intellectual property has likewise emerged as a critical component of modern estates. Authors, artists, musicians, and inventors often generate royalty streams that can endure long after their deaths. Trusts can be structured to manage these intangible assets, ensuring steady income for beneficiaries and safeguarding intellectual property rights in perpetuity. In an economy increasingly driven by creativity and innovation, this function of trusts has grown indispensable.

Risk management represents the third pillar of modern trust integration. Life insurance trusts are a well-established example, allowing the proceeds of a policy to be excluded from taxable estates while providing liquidity for heirs. By holding the policy within a trust, families can ensure that beneficiaries receive maximum value without erosion from estate taxes. Disability income replacement is another growing application, particularly as individuals recognize the financial impact of long-term incapacity. Trust-owned policies can fund distributions to maintain a beneficiary's standard of living in such circumstances. Similarly, the rising cost of long-term care has made insurance coordination with trusts a critical priority. Policies covering assisted living, home care, or nursing facilities can be integrated with trust distributions, creating a comprehensive safety net that shields both beneficiaries and estate assets from being consumed by healthcare expenses.

Taken together, these integrations mark a decisive shift in how trusts function in modern financial life. They are no longer passive repositories of wealth but active managers of diverse, complex, and often intangible assets. By embracing technology, alternative investments, and risk-mitigating insurance strategies, trusts embody the principle of resilience that has characterized their history from medieval times to the digital era. Their enduring relevance lies in this ability to evolve, aligning ancient principles of fiduciary stewardship with the demands of a rapidly changing world.

Chapter 2: Revocable vs. Irrevocable Trusts — Strategic Decision Framework

"In preparing for battle, I have always found that plans are useless, but planning is indispensable." — Dwight D. Eisenhower

The trust is one of the most versatile legal tools available to individuals seeking to preserve, manage, and distribute wealth. Yet its versatility also presents a fundamental choice at the outset: whether to establish a revocable or an irrevocable trust. Each carries distinct implications for flexibility, taxation, asset protection, and long-term legacy planning. Understanding these implications is not an academic exercise but a practical necessity, as the decision shapes how one's wealth interacts with creditors, tax authorities, and future generations. The Internal Revenue Service, which processes over 3.2 million trust tax returns annually, has observed that approximately 89% of new trust formations are revocable. This statistic reflects a broad preference for control and adaptability. However, irrevocable trusts continue to play a critical role in advanced estate planning, particularly where tax mitigation and asset protection are paramount.

The challenge for any planner, therefore, lies not in deciding whether trusts are valuable—they clearly are—but in discerning which type of trust aligns with the grantor's objectives. A well-crafted strategy requires weighing the flexibility of revocable structures against the potential tax benefits and creditor protections of irrevocable arrangements. The following section outlines this analysis in depth, beginning with grantor control mechanisms, moving through the trade-offs in asset protection, and concluding with estate tax inclusion considerations.

2.1 Flexibility Versus Tax Benefits Analysis Matrix

Grantor Control Retention Mechanisms

The primary attraction of a revocable trust lies in the degree of control it affords the grantor during life. At its core, a revocable trust allows the creator to amend, revoke, or restate its provisions at any time, so long as they remain competent to do so. This power extends to altering beneficiaries, adjusting distribution schedules, or changing trustees if circumstances demand. The ability to revoke ensures that the grantor is never locked into a framework that no longer reflects their priorities. For families navigating marriages, divorces, births, or evolving financial conditions, such flexibility is invaluable.

From a tax perspective, revocable trusts are also attractive because they are treated as "grantor trusts" for income tax purposes. This means that all income, deductions, and credits flow directly to the grantor's individual return, avoiding the need for a separate trust return during the grantor's lifetime. The simplicity of this arrangement minimizes administrative costs and reduces the complexity of reporting. Importantly, it ensures that trust income is taxed at the individual's marginal rate rather than the compressed brackets applied to non-grantor trusts, which reach the highest federal rate with comparatively little income.

Control within a revocable trust extends beyond mere amendment powers. Grantors often retain the right to manage investments, either directly or through delegated authority. This capacity allows them to direct portfolio allocations, oversee real estate holdings, or manage closely held business interests within the trust. They can also exercise discretion in making distributions, either by instructing the trustee or by serving as their own trustee, provided they comply with fiduciary standards. In practice, this means that for most individuals, life continues much as it did before funding the trust, with the added benefit of streamlined succession upon incapacity or death.

Yet it is precisely this retention of control that limits the revocable trust's protective power. Because the grantor retains ownership for tax and creditor purposes, assets in a revocable trust remain subject to estate inclusion and personal liability. The IRS, creditors, and courts treat these assets as though they are still personally owned, which sets the stage for a key trade-off.

Trade-offs in Asset Protection Capabilities

While revocable trusts excel in flexibility, they offer little in the way of asset protection during the grantor's lifetime. Creditors can reach the trust's assets to satisfy claims against the grantor, and in many states, even the bankruptcy court may include them in proceedings. This reality makes revocable trusts unsuitable as standalone tools for shielding wealth from lawsuits, divorce settlements, or other financial risks.

That said, the calculus changes upon the grantor's death. Once the revocable trust becomes irrevocable, its provisions solidify, and the assets it contains can be structured to provide meaningful protection for beneficiaries. Spendthrift clauses, discretionary distribution standards, and trustee oversight can all ensure that beneficiaries enjoy the benefits of inheritance without exposing assets to their personal creditors. In this way, revocable trusts provide a two-phase strategy: minimal protection for the grantor during life but enhanced safeguards for heirs thereafter.

For individuals seeking stronger protection during life, irrevocable trusts become essential. By relinquishing the right to revoke or amend, the grantor effectively surrenders ownership, placing the assets beyond the reach of personal creditors and outside the taxable estate. This sacrifice of control, however, comes at the cost of flexibility. Once assets are placed in an irrevocable trust, the grantor cannot easily retrieve or repurpose them. For this reason, careful timing becomes a critical element of strategy. Some grantors establish revocable trusts initially, enjoying the benefits of control, and then later convert or "decant" assets into irrevocable structures as circumstances warrant. This staged approach allows them to balance adaptability with protection, aligning their estate plan with evolving priorities and risk profiles.

Estate Tax Inclusion Implications

The decision between revocable and irrevocable trusts is most starkly felt in the realm of estate taxation. Under Sections 2036 and 2038 of the Internal Revenue Code, assets in a revocable trust are included in the grantor's gross estate because the grantor retains the power to alter, amend, or revoke. As a result, these assets are fully subject to estate tax at death, reducing the net value passed to heirs if the estate exceeds federal or state exemption thresholds.

Irrevocable trusts, by contrast, remove assets from the taxable estate once properly established and funded. By relinquishing control, the grantor ensures that appreciation and income generated within the trust accrue outside their estate, potentially saving substantial amounts in estate taxes. However, this advantage must be weighed against the permanence of the decision, as the grantor cannot later reclaim assets should personal needs arise.

Sophisticated planners often employ hybrid strategies to mitigate this dilemma. For instance, grantors may use irrevocable life insurance trusts to exclude policy proceeds from the estate while retaining liquid assets in revocable trusts for personal use. Similarly, spousal lifetime access trusts (SLATs) allow one spouse to place assets in an irrevocable trust for the benefit of the other, thereby removing them from the estate while preserving indirect access. Such structures illustrate how irrevocable trusts can achieve tax efficiency without entirely abandoning flexibility.

Another dimension involves the generation-skipping transfer tax (GSTT), which applies to transfers that "skip" a generation, such as gifts to grandchildren. Properly structured irrevocable trusts can leverage GSTT exemptions to establish multi-generational wealth vehicles, ensuring that assets benefit not just children but also grandchildren and great-grandchildren without incurring repeated estate taxation at each generational level. Revocable trusts, by contrast, do not confer such advantages until they become irrevocable, making them less effective tools for dynasty planning unless paired with other instruments.

2.2 Conversion Strategies and Timing Optimization

The decision to shift assets from a revocable to an irrevocable trust rarely occurs in a single stroke. Instead, it is a process that requires both foresight and timing, as the advantages of irrevocability—chiefly tax efficiency and asset protection—are counterbalanced by the permanent loss of control. Modern estate planning acknowledges that life does not unfold predictably. Families change, health deteriorates, markets fluctuate, and legislation evolves. Consequently, planners have developed a range of conversion strategies designed to allow individuals to gradually surrender control at moments when doing so creates maximum benefit and minimal sacrifice.

One increasingly common approach is the use of partial irrevocability techniques. Rather than forcing the grantor into an all-or-nothing decision, hybrid structures are crafted to combine revocable and irrevocable elements within the same estate plan. For instance, a revocable trust might serve as the central repository for most assets, providing flexibility during life. From this base, funds can be directed into an irrevocable life insurance trust (ILIT) designed to remove the death benefit of a policy from the taxable estate. Because life insurance proceeds can dramatically inflate an estate's value, isolating them in an irrevocable vehicle ensures liquidity for heirs without subjecting them to estate tax. Another method involves using powers of appointment within irrevocable trusts. By granting a trusted individual the authority to redirect certain distributions or designate contingent beneficiaries, planners inject a degree of flexibility into an otherwise rigid arrangement. These techniques reflect a recognition that irrevocability need not mean absolute rigidity, and that carefully drafted provisions can preserve adaptability without undermining the protective power of the structure.

Health considerations often act as catalysts for conversion. A medical diagnosis or a decline in capacity can prompt families to act quickly, moving assets into irrevocable trusts before opportunities are lost. Long-term care planning is particularly relevant here. In the United States, Medicaid imposes strict eligibility requirements, including asset limits that can disqualify individuals from receiving benefits. Assets transferred into an irrevocable trust may be excluded from consideration, but only if the transfer occurs outside the so-called "look-back" period, which in most states extends five years. This reality underscores the importance of early action. By converting or funding irrevocable trusts well in advance of a medical crisis, families can protect homes and savings from being consumed by long-term care costs. At the same time, incapacity planning requires structures that ensure continuity without unnecessary court involvement. Revocable trusts often serve as the initial framework, allowing for easy management during health challenges, but targeted conversions at the right moment can fortify protections when vulnerability increases.

Economic cycles also play a pivotal role in timing conversions. Market downturns, though often feared, can present unique opportunities for estate planning. When asset values are depressed, transferring them into irrevocable trusts locks in lower valuations for tax purposes. If those assets subsequently recover in value, the appreciation occurs outside the taxable estate, amplifying the tax efficiency of the strategy. Similarly, interest rate environments influence the effectiveness of certain vehicles, such as grantor retained annuity trusts (GRATs). Low interest rates reduce the annuity payments required to satisfy IRS assumptions, allowing more appreciation to escape taxation. Conversely, in high interest rate environments, other strategies may prove more advantageous. Legislative changes also create windows of opportunity. The federal estate tax exemption, for example, has historically fluctuated with political priorities. Families who anticipate reductions in the exemption may choose to accelerate conversions, locking in higher exemptions before they expire. In this sense, estate planning is not static but reactive, requiring attentiveness to both personal milestones and macroeconomic conditions.

Together, these strategies illustrate that the path from revocability to irrevocability is not a cliff but a continuum. Families can move assets incrementally, triggered by health events, market dynamics, or legislative deadlines. By aligning conversions with the rhythms of life and the economy, planners ensure that the surrender of control is not an arbitrary sacrifice but a calculated decision that maximizes protection and efficiency.

2.3 Advanced Hybrid Structures and Innovative Approaches

The interplay between revocable and irrevocable trusts has inspired a host of advanced strategies that push beyond conventional estate planning. These innovations recognize that no two families are alike, and that wealth management is as much about governance and relationships as it is about legal formality. Modern planners increasingly draw on tools such as decanting, multi-jurisdictional planning, and family office integration to build trust structures that are as flexible and resilient as the families they serve.

Decanting has emerged as one of the most powerful tools for modernizing and adapting existing trusts. Much like pouring wine from one bottle into another, decanting allows trustees to transfer assets from an outdated trust into a new one with improved provisions. This process can be judicial, requiring court approval, or non-judicial, relying on statutory authority and trustee discretion, depending on the state. Through decanting, families can address tax law changes, add special needs provisions, or modify distribution standards to better reflect current realities. Some states grant broad decanting powers, allowing nearly wholesale rewriting of terms, while others impose stricter limits. Beneficiary consent and virtual representation mechanisms further enhance flexibility by ensuring that all interested parties, including minors or unborn descendants, are represented in the process. Decanting not only breathes new life into aging trusts but also underscores the adaptability of trust law to evolving family and financial landscapes.

Multi-jurisdictional trust planning has become equally vital in an era of mobility and interstate competition. Not all states treat trusts equally, and situs selection—the decision of where a trust is legally domiciled—can profoundly influence outcomes. States such as Nevada, Delaware, and South Dakota have cultivated reputations as trust-friendly jurisdictions, offering advantages like no state income tax, extended perpetuities periods for dynasty trusts, and robust asset protection statutes. A family might migrate an existing trust to one of these jurisdictions to take advantage of superior laws, or they may establish new trusts there from the outset. Provisions for changing governing law allow families to adjust situs as their needs evolve, ensuring access to favorable frameworks even if they reside elsewhere. In a world where wealth frequently crosses borders, this ability to strategically locate trusts has become an indispensable component of high-level estate planning.

Beyond legal mechanics, advanced planning increasingly incorporates family governance. Trusts, after all, are not just about transferring assets—they are about transmitting values. Family office integration provides a model for aligning trust purposes with broader governance structures. Families may establish written constitutions that articulate their shared principles, investment philosophies, and philanthropic commitments. These constitutions serve as guiding documents for trustees and beneficiaries alike, ensuring that the trust functions not merely as a financial vehicle but as a reflection of collective identity.

Preparing the next generation has become a cornerstone of this approach. Trusts can incorporate educational components, requiring beneficiaries to complete financial literacy programs or participate in family meetings before receiving distributions. By embedding education into the trust's structure, families cultivate stewards rather than passive recipients, empowering future generations to sustain wealth rather than squander it.

Conflict resolution mechanisms are also increasingly recognized as essential. Disputes over trusts can fracture families, eroding both wealth and relationships. To mitigate this risk, some trusts now include mediation protocols, appointing neutral advisors to facilitate dialogue when disagreements arise. By formalizing processes for resolving conflict, these provisions safeguard not only financial assets but also family harmony.

The integration of governance, jurisdictional flexibility, and decanting strategies reveals the cutting edge of estate planning. Trusts are no longer static repositories of wealth bound by the rigid terms of centuries past. They are dynamic frameworks capable of evolving with markets, laws, and family dynamics. Advanced hybrid structures embody this evolution, demonstrating that estate planning is not just about avoiding taxes or probate but about building legacies that endure in substance and spirit.

Chapter 3: Advanced Funding Strategies and Asset Allocation

"Risk comes from not knowing what you're doing." — Warren Buffett

The creation of a trust is only the beginning of a successful estate plan. Its true effectiveness is determined not by the elegance of its drafting, but by the diligence with which it is funded. A revocable trust, no matter how well structured, remains a hollow vessel until assets are properly transferred into it. Data demonstrates this with striking clarity: properly funded revocable trusts reduce estate administration costs by sixty to eighty percent compared to probate proceedings, saving families between fifty thousand and two hundred thousand dollars per estate. These savings are not only financial; they also represent time, privacy, and peace of mind for heirs who would otherwise be mired in bureaucratic delays and public scrutiny. Strategic funding and thoughtful asset allocation ensure that the trust fulfills its promise of efficiency, protection, and legacy preservation.

Funding, however, is not a mechanical exercise. Each class of asset brings unique legal, tax, and practical considerations that determine how it should be transferred, titled, and managed within the trust. Real estate, business interests, financial accounts, and insurance policies require distinct approaches, and missteps can undermine the very goals the trust was designed to achieve. Strategic asset selection, therefore, is both an art and a science. It requires balancing liquidity with growth, security with opportunity, and tax efficiency with operational practicality.

3.1 Strategic Asset Selection for Trust Funding

Real estate has long been at the heart of estate planning, not only because it often represents the most valuable component of a family's wealth but also because it carries layers of symbolic meaning. Homes anchor family identity, while investment properties generate income streams that sustain future generations. Transferring real estate into a trust requires careful attention to title and deed preparation. The process typically involves executing a new deed naming the trust as owner, but the specific requirements vary by jurisdiction. Errors in recording or drafting can cloud title and complicate later transfers. Furthermore, property tax implications must be addressed, especially in states that grant homestead exemptions. In some jurisdictions, transferring a residence into a revocable trust does not affect the exemption, but in others, improper handling can lead to its loss, increasing annual tax burdens. Beyond tax treatment, the trust must also account for liabilities arising from real estate ownership. Rental properties, for example, expose owners to risks of tenant disputes, injuries, and lawsuits. Structuring these assets within the trust may involve layering them through limited liability companies that are in turn owned by the trust, isolating liabilities while preserving centralized management. In this way, real estate funding is not simply about transferring a deed but about weaving together tax planning, liability management, and long-term property stewardship.

Business interests present an entirely different set of challenges and opportunities. Unlike real estate, which is tangible and relatively stable, closely held businesses embody dynamic enterprises that depend on governance documents, valuation standards, and the skills of those who manage them. When transferring ownership interests in partnerships, corporations, or limited liability companies to a trust, valuation becomes critical. Minority discounts often apply to non-controlling interests, reducing their taxable value and enhancing estate planning efficiency. However, these discounts must be carefully justified and documented to withstand scrutiny from tax authorities. Operating agreements or shareholder agreements may need modification to recognize trust ownership, ensuring that the trustee can exercise voting rights, receive distributions, and comply with transfer restrictions. A poorly drafted or outdated agreement can inadvertently block trust funding, leaving business interests outside the estate plan's protective framework.

Succession planning further complicates matters. A business is not merely an asset to be transferred; it is an ongoing concern with employees, customers, and partners who depend on its stability. Trust funding must therefore align with buy-sell agreements, which govern the transfer of interests upon death, disability, or retirement of an owner. Coordinating these documents ensures that the trust can either retain ownership or liquidate the interest under favorable terms. Without such integration, the death of a principal could spark disputes among surviving partners, jeopardize continuity, or trigger unwanted liquidation. By embedding business interests into the trust in a coordinated manner, families secure both financial value and organizational resilience, transforming succession from a moment of vulnerability into an orderly transition.

Financial accounts and investment portfolios represent another cornerstone of trust funding. These assets range from retirement accounts and brokerage portfolios to bank deposits and insurance policies, each governed by unique rules. Retirement accounts such as IRAs and 401(k)s require particular caution, as they operate primarily through beneficiary designations. Transferring ownership of these accounts directly into a trust can trigger unintended tax consequences, such as accelerated distributions or loss of favorable "stretch" provisions for beneficiaries. A more effective strategy often involves designating the trust itself as the beneficiary, structured in compliance with Internal Revenue Code requirements to qualify as a "see-through" trust. This allows distributions to be based on the life expectancy of underlying beneficiaries, preserving tax deferral while aligning retirement wealth with broader estate planning objectives.

Taxable investment accounts, by contrast, can generally be retitled in the name of the trust without adverse consequences. Timing and documentation are key, as incomplete transfers may leave accounts vulnerable to probate despite the existence of the trust. Trustees must also consider portfolio management philosophies, ensuring that asset allocation within the trust reflects both risk tolerance and the fiduciary duty to act in the beneficiaries' best interests. Some grantors prefer to appoint professional trustees or financial advisors to oversee investment strategies, ensuring continuity and disciplined management across generations.

Insurance policies occupy a unique niche within trust funding, bridging the gap between liquidity and tax efficiency. Life insurance provides immediate cash flow at death, which can be used to pay estate taxes, equalize inheritances, or provide for dependents. When policies are owned outright by the grantor, proceeds may be included in the taxable estate, reducing their efficiency. By transferring ownership to a trust—often an irrevocable life insurance trust (ILIT)—families exclude these proceeds from estate taxation, preserving their full value for beneficiaries. However, timing is critical, as transfers within three years of death may still draw the proceeds back into the estate under federal tax rules. Trust ownership also requires ongoing premium payments, which must be managed carefully to avoid unintended gift tax consequences. Coordinating insurance funding with other assets ensures that liquidity is available without undermining the overall tax strategy.

Taken together, these categories illustrate the layered complexity of strategic asset selection for trust funding. Real estate demands attention to deeds, tax exemptions, and liability structures. Business interests require valuation discipline, document coordination, and succession foresight. Financial accounts necessitate careful navigation of beneficiary designations and tax implications, while insurance policies call for precision in ownership and premium funding. No single template suffices; each family must align its trust funding strategy with its unique asset mix, financial goals, and legacy aspirations.

The ultimate goal of funding is not merely to fill a legal container with assets but to construct an integrated system that operates efficiently across generations. When done properly, a trust is more than a static repository; it is an engine of continuity, translating wealth into security, opportunity, and stability for heirs. The striking cost savings associated with funded trusts highlight their tangible benefits, but the deeper value lies in their ability to simplify transitions, reduce conflict, and preserve dignity in moments of loss. Strategic funding, in this sense, is not simply about avoiding probate—it is about honoring the work of a lifetime by ensuring it passes forward intact, protected, and aligned with the vision of its creator.

3.2 Tax-Efficient Funding Methodologies

A trust is more than a vessel for assets; it is a platform for orchestrating sophisticated strategies that maximize wealth preservation while minimizing the erosive impact of taxation. Tax efficiency, when woven into the funding process, can significantly enhance the long-term benefits of the trust for its beneficiaries. Properly executed, tax planning does not merely defer obligations but reshapes how wealth is transferred, ensuring that appreciation, income, and distributions accrue in ways that serve both fiscal prudence and family continuity.

One of the most versatile tools in this arena is the grantor trust. When a trust is structured to qualify as a grantor trust for income tax purposes, the grantor is responsible for paying the income taxes on trust earnings, even though the income itself remains within the trust. While this may appear to place an additional burden on the grantor, it is in fact a powerful wealth transfer technique. By paying income tax from their own resources, the grantor effectively reduces their taxable estate without triggering a gift. At the same time, the trust grows unencumbered by tax obligations, compounding wealth for the beneficiaries. The Internal Revenue Service views this arrangement as neutral, but families understand its practical advantage: each dollar the grantor pays in income tax outside the trust is a dollar that remains sheltered and growing within the trust.

This principle can be expanded through installment sales to intentionally defective grantor trusts. Appreciated assets, such as shares in a closely held business, can be sold to the trust in exchange for a promissory note. Because the trust is disregarded for income tax purposes, the sale does not trigger capital gains tax. The assets then appreciate inside the trust, outside the grantor's estate, while the note is repaid over time. If structured properly, this allows wealth to shift to the next generation at discounted values, while avoiding immediate tax recognition.

Charitable planning further enriches these methodologies. A charitable remainder trust (CRT), for instance, allows a grantor to transfer appreciated assets into a trust that provides an income stream either to themselves or to beneficiaries for a term of years or for life. At the conclusion of that period, the remainder passes to a designated charity. The grantor benefits from a charitable deduction upon funding the trust and avoids immediate recognition of capital gains on the transfer. Meanwhile, the assets inside the CRT can grow tax-deferred, with the trust making annual distributions. By integrating charitable objectives with tax planning, families achieve dual goals of philanthropy and fiscal efficiency, all while reinforcing a legacy of giving.

Beyond income tax strategies, generation-skipping transfer (GST) tax planning plays a critical role in maximizing wealth preservation. The GST tax was designed to prevent families from avoiding estate taxes by transferring assets directly to grandchildren or later descendants, thereby skipping an intermediate layer of taxation. However, careful allocation of GST exemptions can transform this potential liability into an opportunity. By allocating GST exemption to properly structured trusts, planners ensure that assets can pass through multiple generations without incurring estate or GST taxes at each level.

The mechanics of this planning often involve distinguishing between direct skips, taxable distributions, and taxable terminations. A direct skip occurs when assets pass directly to a "skip person," such as a grandchild, and triggers immediate GST tax if no exemption is allocated. Taxable distributions and terminations occur later, when non-skip beneficiaries no longer have interests. Optimizing how and when GST exemptions are applied ensures that the trust grows unfettered by repeated taxation, compounding wealth across time horizons that extend well beyond the original grantor. Dynasty trusts, established in jurisdictions that allow perpetual or near-perpetual duration, are particularly effective in this context. By funding a dynasty trust with sufficient exemption allocation, families can create enduring vehicles that sustain wealth for centuries, immune from estate taxation so long as state law permits.

In an increasingly globalized world, tax-efficient funding must also grapple with international considerations. Many families hold assets abroad, whether in foreign bank accounts, investment funds, or real property. U.S. citizens and residents are subject to extensive reporting requirements for such holdings, including the obligation to disclose foreign accounts under the FBAR (Foreign Bank Account Report) regime. Failure to comply can result in penalties that exceed the value of the accounts themselves, making trust integration vital for compliance.

Foreign investments bring further complexity when they involve passive foreign investment companies (PFICs), which impose punitive taxation on U.S. taxpayers unless carefully managed.

Structuring PFIC holdings within trusts requires careful attention to elections and reporting, as improper handling can undermine both tax efficiency and overall wealth objectives.

Pre-immigration trust planning is another critical element for non-U.S. persons who anticipate relocating to the United States. By funding trusts prior to acquiring U.S. tax residency, individuals can shield existing wealth from U.S. estate and gift tax exposure. These pre-immigration trusts act as barriers, ensuring that the new resident's taxable estate encompasses only assets acquired after arrival. Such planning requires precision, as timing is paramount and improper execution can expose families to unintended liabilities.

Tax-efficient funding methodologies thus embody the fusion of technical tax law, strategic foresight, and global awareness. When integrated thoughtfully, they elevate the trust from a static container of wealth to a dynamic engine of multigenerational prosperity, simultaneously reducing liabilities and aligning financial stewardship with family objectives.

3.3 Dynamic Asset Management and Rebalancing Strategies

Funding a trust is not a one-time act but the beginning of an ongoing relationship between assets, beneficiaries, and fiduciaries. Wealth, once placed within a trust, must continue to grow, adapt, and respond to changing circumstances. Dynamic asset management is therefore essential, ensuring that trust portfolios remain aligned with both the financial objectives of the grantor and the evolving needs of beneficiaries. This process requires attentiveness to life cycles, openness to alternative investments, and sensitivity to the social and ethical dimensions of investing.

Life cycle allocation models offer one framework for dynamic management. Just as individual investors adjust their portfolios as they move from youth to retirement, trusts too must evolve based on the life stages of their beneficiaries. A trust established for young children may initially emphasize growth-oriented investments, accepting higher risk in anticipation of long time horizons. As those children mature and require funds for education, marriage, or home ownership, allocations may shift toward income generation or liquidity. Later, as beneficiaries approach their own retirement years, a trust might further rebalance toward stability and preservation, reducing exposure to volatility. Trustees, bound by fiduciary duties, must balance these shifts against the overarching intent of the trust, ensuring that allocations reflect not just market conditions but the timing and nature of beneficiary needs.

Alternative investments add another dimension to this management process. Traditional portfolios built on stocks and bonds may not provide sufficient diversification or yield, particularly in low-interest-rate environments. Trusts increasingly incorporate alternative assets such as private placements, hedge funds, or direct real estate holdings. These instruments can offer higher returns, but they also demand sophisticated oversight and a clear understanding of suitability. Trustees must carefully evaluate the liquidity, transparency, and risk profiles of such investments, recognizing that the fiduciary standard requires prudence rather than speculation.

Real estate investments illustrate this tension well. While direct ownership of property offers tangible security and potential income, it also imposes management burdens and liability risks. Real estate investment trusts (REITs), by contrast, provide exposure to property markets without the operational demands, offering greater liquidity and diversification. Trustees must weigh these trade-offs, considering whether beneficiaries are best served by the steady dividends of REITs or the potential appreciation and control of direct holdings.

Commodities and precious metals introduce further options, often functioning as hedges against inflation or geopolitical uncertainty. Allocating a portion of trust portfolios to gold, silver, or energy commodities can stabilize returns during turbulent markets, but overexposure risks reducing growth potential. The challenge lies in finding the equilibrium that provides both resilience and opportunity, consistent with the trust's purpose.

In recent years, environmental, social, and governance (ESG) criteria have transformed how trusts approach investment. Families increasingly demand that their wealth not only grow but also reflect their values. Trustees respond by screening investments through ESG frameworks, avoiding companies with poor environmental records or weak governance practices while prioritizing those that align with sustainability. This approach, known as mission-related or impact investing, aligns the financial strategy of the trust with the ethical commitments of the family. Trusts may, for instance, invest in renewable energy projects, socially responsible enterprises, or funds that measure impact alongside profit.

Importantly, ESG investing does not mean abandoning performance. Studies increasingly suggest that companies with strong ESG practices often outperform peers in the long run, benefiting from resilience, innovation, and reputational strength. By integrating ESG principles, trustees not only honor the values of the family but also position portfolios for sustainable growth. Impact measurement and reporting further reinforce this alignment, providing transparency about how investments achieve both financial returns and social good.

Dynamic asset management, therefore, transcends mere rebalancing. It is a continuous dialogue between market forces, fiduciary obligations, and human values. Trustees must remain vigilant, flexible, and responsive, ensuring that trust portfolios remain vibrant, diversified, and purposeful. In doing so, they transform the trust from a static inheritance vehicle into a living institution, capable of adapting to shifting markets, evolving beneficiaries, and emerging ethical imperatives.

Chapter 4: Trustee Selection and Governance Optimization

"The greatest compliment that was ever paid me was when someone asked me what I think, and attended to my answer." —
Henry David Thoreau

The decision of who should serve as trustee is among the most consequential choices in estate planning. A trust is only as effective as the individual or institution entrusted with its administration, and the stakes are high. Trustees not only manage assets but also interpret intent, balance competing interests, and make decisions that reverberate across generations. Governance optimization ensures that these decisions are carried out faithfully, prudently, and transparently. Yet the statistics highlight a paradox: family trustees often spark conflict—70% of trusts managed by relatives experience disputes—while professional trustees reduce conflict to 23%. At the same time, family involvement raises beneficiary satisfaction by 40%, underscoring that trust administration is as much about relationships as it is about fiduciary rigor. Striking the right balance requires a framework for evaluating professional trustees that goes beyond surface-level credentials and dives into their financial stability, service models, and jurisdictional competencies.

4.1 Professional Trustee Evaluation Framework

When families consider appointing professional trustees, institutional options often appear first. Large banks and trust companies advertise themselves as reliable, neutral, and well-capitalized. Yet not all institutions are created equal, and due diligence is essential to determine whether their strengths align with the needs of the trust. A thorough evaluation begins with financial stability. Trustees hold not only fiduciary responsibility but also, in many cases, custody of significant assets. The collapse of an institution, or even its exposure to regulatory sanctions, can place those assets at risk or disrupt administration. Families must therefore examine the institution's balance sheet, capitalization levels, and credit ratings. Regulatory compliance history also provides a crucial lens: past violations or litigation may reveal systemic weaknesses in governance. An institution with a spotless compliance record signals not only financial prudence but also a culture of accountability, both of which are indispensable for trusteeship.

Investment management capabilities stand at the heart of professional trusteeship. Families often turn to institutional trustees precisely because they offer access to sophisticated portfolio management, research, and risk analysis. Yet here, too, scrutiny is necessary. Institutions vary widely in track record, with some outperforming benchmarks consistently while others simply mirror the market at elevated fees. Families must weigh whether the trustee employs an active or passive strategy, whether it can tailor allocations to unique family goals, and how it measures and communicates performance. Fee structures require particular attention. While a flat annual fee based on assets under management may appear straightforward, hidden costs can accumulate through transaction charges, fund expenses, or layered advisory fees. A professional trustee whose compensation is transparent, competitive, and aligned with the beneficiaries' interests is far more likely to foster trust and avoid future disputes.

In today's world, technology plays as significant a role in fiduciary service as financial acumen. Beneficiaries expect transparency, real-time access, and responsive communication. Institutions that provide robust online platforms, with dashboards that track investments, distributions, and tax reporting, empower families with visibility and accountability. Conversely, outdated systems or opaque reporting can create frustration and suspicion. The ability to deliver services digitally has become even more critical in the wake of global disruptions such as the COVID-19 pandemic, when physical access to offices was curtailed. Trustees who deploy secure digital communication and document management systems not only enhance efficiency but also demonstrate resilience in adapting to modern expectations.

While institutions bring scale and infrastructure, boutique trust companies offer a compelling alternative. These smaller firms often position themselves as providers of personalized service, tailoring their administration to the nuances of each family. Unlike large banks, which may rotate staff or rely on standardized procedures, boutique trustees often cultivate long-term relationships, learning the family's history, values, and dynamics. This relational continuity can mitigate the perception of detachment that sometimes accompanies institutional trusteeship. Moreover, boutique firms may specialize in unique asset classes—such as family-owned businesses, agricultural holdings, or complex real estate portfolios—that demand expertise beyond the scope of mass-market institutions. For entrepreneurial families or those with unconventional wealth structures, such specialization can prove invaluable.

The integration of boutique trustees into family office arrangements further strengthens their appeal. By collaborating with advisors, accountants, and attorneys already familiar with the family, boutique trustees can embed themselves within a broader governance framework, creating cohesion across all aspects of financial and legacy planning. Yet boutique trustees also present limitations. Their smaller scale can restrict resources, making them more vulnerable to market shifts or operational risks. Their fee structures may be higher relative to institutions, reflecting the cost of specialized and personalized service. Families must weigh whether the incremental benefits of tailored administration justify the potential trade-offs in stability and cost efficiency.

Geographic considerations add another layer of complexity. Trusts are creatures of state law, and the jurisdiction—or situs—chosen for administration can materially influence outcomes. States like Delaware, Nevada, and South Dakota have cultivated trust-friendly statutes that extend the duration of trusts, enhance asset protection, and minimize state-level income taxation. Selecting a trustee domiciled in one of these jurisdictions can unlock significant advantages, but it also requires careful coordination to ensure that the situs aligns with family needs and federal tax obligations. A professional trustee located in a favorable jurisdiction may offer opportunities that a local trustee cannot.

Remote administration capabilities increasingly allow families to access these jurisdictional benefits without being geographically tethered. Professional trustees with robust digital infrastructure can manage trusts seamlessly across state lines, providing real-time service regardless of physical location. Still, interstate administration can spark conflicts of law, particularly when beneficiaries or assets are located in multiple jurisdictions. Professional trustees must therefore demonstrate expertise in navigating interstate issues, ensuring that the trust's governing law prevails and that conflicting claims are resolved efficiently.

Ultimately, evaluating professional trustees requires more than comparing fee schedules or brand names. It is a holistic process that examines financial strength, investment acumen, technological capability, service model, and jurisdictional expertise. Families must ask whether the trustee can preserve not only the trust's assets but also its purpose, balancing technical precision with sensitivity to relationships. The statistics underscore the stakes: professional trustees may reduce conflict but risk alienating beneficiaries if perceived as impersonal, while family trustees may engender satisfaction but fuel disputes. The most effective governance frameworks often blend professional oversight with family involvement, ensuring both rigor and resonance.

By applying a rigorous evaluation framework, families position themselves to select trustees who not only manage wealth competently but also cultivate trust in the broader sense—trust in their fairness, reliability, and commitment to the family's vision. In this way, trustee selection becomes not merely an administrative decision but an act of legacy, ensuring that governance reflects both the letter of the law and the spirit of the family it serves.

4.2 Family Trustee Integration and Training Programs

The decision to appoint family members as trustees is often rooted in values of loyalty, intimacy, and trust in the personal sense of the word. A family trustee brings a sense of connection that no institution can replicate, ensuring that decisions are made by someone who understands the personalities, histories, and needs of the beneficiaries. Yet these appointments also introduce significant risks. Fiduciary duties are demanding, financial literacy is uneven, and the legal framework that governs trusteeship is complex. Without proper training and governance structures, family trustees may unintentionally mismanage assets, violate fiduciary obligations, or fuel conflicts. The solution lies not in excluding family involvement but in creating robust integration and training programs that transform well-intentioned but inexperienced relatives into capable fiduciaries.

Preparing the next generation of family trustees is an endeavor that begins long before formal appointment. Families committed to continuity recognize that financial literacy must be cultivated from an early stage. Education in investment principles, accounting basics, and estate law equips younger family members with the competence to engage meaningfully when their turn comes. Workshops on fiduciary responsibility provide exposure to the standards of loyalty, prudence, and impartiality that underpin trustee obligations. By embedding this education within the family culture, potential trustees internalize not just technical knowledge but also the ethical gravity of their role. Mentorship programs, in which emerging trustees shadow experienced professional fiduciaries, provide invaluable practical exposure. Observing how seasoned trustees evaluate investment strategies, resolve conflicts, or interpret trust provisions bridges the gap between theory and practice, creating a lineage of competency that endures across generations.

Co-trustee structures add another layer of resilience by balancing family involvement with professional expertise. Families often appoint one relative and one institutional trustee to serve jointly, ensuring that intimate knowledge of family dynamics is complemented by technical skill. The division of responsibilities must be clearly articulated to avoid duplication or neglect. For instance, the professional trustee might oversee investment management and compliance, while the family trustee provides input on beneficiary needs and approves discretionary distributions. This structure preserves the human element without compromising fiduciary rigor. Yet co-trusteeship also risks deadlock, particularly when disagreements arise over distributions or investment strategies. Mechanisms for tie-breaking are therefore essential. Some trusts appoint a third co-trustee with limited authority to cast deciding votes, while others mandate mediation or arbitration before disputes escalate. Regular communication protocols, such as quarterly family meetings and documented minutes, provide transparency and accountability, ensuring that all voices are heard and that decisions reflect both professional standards and family values.

Succession planning for family trustees is perhaps the most delicate yet vital element of governance. Identifying and preparing successor trustees requires foresight, as illness, incapacity, or simple disinterest can create unexpected vacancies. Families must therefore establish pipelines for training, ensuring that younger generations are equipped and willing to assume responsibility when needed. Transition planning should include structured handovers, where outgoing trustees gradually transfer authority while mentoring their replacements. Knowledge transfer is critical, encompassing not only financial data and legal documents but also the subtler aspects of family dynamics and values that guide decision-making.

Accountability mechanisms must also exist for instances where family trustees underperform. While removal may be emotionally fraught, failing to address incompetence can erode both trust assets and family harmony. Performance evaluations, whether conducted internally or by independent advisors, allow families to assess whether trustees are fulfilling their fiduciary duties effectively. Removal provisions, carefully drafted into the trust, provide a safety valve by permitting substitution without protracted litigation. In this way, succession and oversight ensure that family involvement strengthens rather than undermines governance, creating a sustainable model of shared stewardship across generations.

4.3 Trust Governance Innovation and Best Practices

As trusts grow in size and complexity, traditional models of trustee authority often prove insufficient. Families increasingly recognize that governance must evolve to incorporate specialized expertise, technological innovation, and systematic accountability. The goal is not only to preserve wealth but to do so in ways that are transparent, adaptive, and aligned with long-term objectives. Emerging best practices in trust governance point toward a model that blends fiduciary rigor with collaborative structures and modern tools.

One of the most significant innovations is the use of advisory and distribution committees. Rather than relying solely on trustees, families appoint committees composed of individuals with specialized knowledge. A trust advisory committee, for instance, may include investment professionals, tax advisors, or family representatives who provide guidance without bearing fiduciary liability. Their recommendations inform trustee decisions, ensuring that complex portfolios benefit from diverse perspectives. Investment committees take this a step further by formalizing oversight of asset allocation, risk management, and performance benchmarking. Distribution committees, meanwhile, establish clear protocols for handling discretionary distributions, reducing the perception of bias or arbitrariness by trustees. When structured thoughtfully, these committees create an ecosystem of shared responsibility that enhances both expertise and legitimacy.

Technology has also revolutionized trust governance. Modern trustees deploy digital platforms that allow beneficiaries to access information securely and transparently. Online portals provide real-time views of account balances, investment performance, and distribution histories, replacing opaque statements with interactive dashboards. Digital signatures and remote meeting capabilities streamline decision-making, allowing trustees and beneficiaries to collaborate regardless of geographic location.

These tools not only enhance efficiency but also reflect the expectations of younger generations accustomed to seamless digital engagement. Yet technology brings risks alongside opportunities. Cybersecurity protocols are essential to safeguard sensitive financial and personal data. Trustees must invest in robust systems that protect against hacking, identity theft, and data breaches, recognizing that breaches can erode both financial stability and familial trust.

Performance measurement is the third pillar of governance innovation. Trustees historically operated with broad discretion, but modern beneficiaries demand transparency and accountability. Establishing key performance indicators for trust administration creates a framework for evaluating effectiveness. Metrics may include investment returns relative to benchmarks, timeliness of distributions, responsiveness to beneficiary inquiries, and compliance with tax obligations. Regular reporting schedules, often quarterly, reinforce accountability by providing beneficiaries with clear and consistent updates. Transparency initiatives go beyond numbers, however, incorporating narrative explanations of decisions and contextualizing performance within the trust's objectives.

Beneficiary feedback mechanisms further strengthen accountability. Trusts are not abstractions; they exist to serve the individuals named within them. Creating formal channels for feedback—whether through surveys, structured interviews, or family forums—ensures that beneficiaries feel heard and valued. While fiduciary duty requires trustees to exercise independent judgment, listening to beneficiary perspectives promotes trust in both senses of the word. Satisfaction measurement becomes as important as financial performance, recognizing that the health of the family dynamic is inseparable from the health of the trust.

Collectively, these innovations represent a shift from static, hierarchical models of governance to dynamic, participatory systems. Advisory committees expand expertise, technology enhances transparency, and performance measurement embeds accountability. Together, they create governance structures that are resilient, responsive, and relational. In this model, trusts are no longer simply legal containers for assets but living institutions that evolve with the families they serve. By embracing innovation and best practices, trustees and beneficiaries alike cultivate a governance culture that honors tradition while embracing modernity, ensuring that wealth endures not just in financial terms but as a foundation for harmony, purpose, and legacy.

Chapter 5: Tax Planning Strategies and Compliance Framework

"The hardest thing in the world to understand is the income tax." — Albert Einstein

Few areas of estate planning provoke as much confusion or anxiety as taxes. Yet it is precisely within this complexity that opportunities emerge for families who approach planning with foresight and precision. The stark reality is that the average American family pays nearly a quarter more in estate-related taxes when assets are funneled through probate rather than carefully structured trusts. That figure reflects not only lost dollars but also lost chances—chances to preserve wealth, support heirs, and build lasting legacies. Properly designed tax planning strategies transform trusts from mere containers of assets into engines of efficiency, allowing families to navigate a system that often feels designed to frustrate rather than facilitate financial stability.

Income tax planning, particularly in the context of grantor trusts, sits at the heart of this effort. While estate and gift taxes typically draw the most attention in popular discussions, income taxes often erode wealth far more consistently over time. A grantor trust, when structured and managed deliberately, becomes a powerful vehicle for aligning income tax liabilities with broader estate planning goals. By shifting who is responsible for paying taxes and how distributions are timed, families can enhance after-tax growth, balance tax burdens across generations, and ensure that wealth is stewarded in ways that maximize both control and compliance.

5.1 Income Tax Optimization for Grantor Trusts

The designation of a trust as a grantor trust under the Internal Revenue Code is not accidental but the result of deliberate planning. When a trust qualifies as a grantor trust, the grantor— the individual who created and funded the trust—remains responsible for paying income taxes on its earnings, even if those earnings are retained within the trust. At first glance, this arrangement may appear counterintuitive. Why should the grantor pay taxes on income they no longer directly enjoy? The answer lies in the wealth transfer benefits. By covering the trust's tax liability from their own resources, the grantor effectively removes additional value from their taxable estate without triggering gift tax consequences. Meanwhile, the trust's assets grow unencumbered, compounding over time and passing more efficiently to beneficiaries. This subtle but potent mechanism allows the grantor to subsidize the growth of the trust, quietly enhancing its long-term value.

Intentional grantor trust status is therefore one of the most common strategies in advanced estate planning. Families with significant taxable estates use it to accelerate the transfer of wealth, particularly when paired with installment sales of appreciating assets. For example, a business owner might sell non-voting shares of a closely held company to an intentionally defective grantor trust in exchange for a promissory note.

Because the trust is disregarded for income tax purposes, the sale itself does not trigger recognition of gain. The business then continues to appreciate inside the trust, while the note payments provide the grantor with cash flow. Over time, the appreciation accrues outside the estate, while the grantor's payment of income taxes effectively serves as an additional transfer of value.

Yet grantor trust status is not always permanent or desirable. Circumstances change, and with them, tax strategies must adapt. High-income grantors may find that the burden of covering the trust's tax liability strains their liquidity, particularly if the trust's investments generate significant taxable income. In such cases, planners may consider strategies to terminate grantor trust status, shifting liability from the individual to the trust itself. This conversion can be triggered by altering powers retained by the grantor, such as removing the right to substitute assets of equal value or terminating certain administrative controls. By switching status at the appropriate time, families maintain flexibility, ensuring that tax burdens are borne where they can be most efficiently managed.

Distribution planning offers another powerful lever for income tax optimization. Trusts are subject to highly compressed tax brackets, reaching the highest federal income tax rate with just a fraction of the income required for individuals. To avoid excessive taxation, trustees can distribute income to beneficiaries, who may be taxed at lower marginal rates. This process, governed by the distributable net income (DNI) rules, allows trusts to pass through income tax liability alongside distributions, creating opportunities for arbitrage between trust and individual rates. Families with multiple beneficiaries in different tax brackets can optimize distributions to achieve maximum efficiency. For example, instead of allowing all income to accumulate within the trust and be taxed at the top rate, the trustee might distribute portions to adult children in lower brackets, thereby reducing overall liability.

Timing also matters. Distributions made before year-end are treated as taxable to beneficiaries in the current year, while those made early in the following year can be carried back if properly designated. Trustees can use this flexibility to balance income recognition across tax years, smoothing liabilities and avoiding spikes. In families where multiple generations are involved, timing strategies can also account for life-stage differences. Younger beneficiaries with lower incomes may be well-positioned to receive taxable distributions, while older beneficiaries nearing retirement may prefer non-taxable distributions of principal. Coordinating distributions in this way transforms tax planning from a reactive obligation into a proactive strategy for enhancing family-wide efficiency.

Investment management within grantor trusts must also align with tax considerations. While the grantor bears responsibility for income taxes, the selection of investments can significantly influence outcomes. Tax-efficient investments, such as index funds with low turnover, minimize annual taxable income while still providing long-term growth. Municipal bonds, exempt from federal income tax and often from state taxes, are particularly attractive for high-net-worth grantors in high-tax jurisdictions. These instruments provide steady income without compounding the tax burden borne by the grantor.

Capital gains planning is equally critical. Trustees and grantors must decide whether to harvest gains strategically, realizing them in years when tax rates are favorable or offset by losses. For instance, if the grantor has other losses outside the trust that can be used to offset gains, realizing appreciation within the trust can be tax-neutral while resetting basis for future growth. Conversely, if capital gains rates are expected to increase due to legislative changes, preemptively realizing gains may lock in lower rates. Such timing requires careful monitoring of both personal circumstances and broader economic trends, underscoring that tax planning is as much about anticipation as it is about compliance.

When these strategies are integrated—grantor trust status management, distribution planning, and tax-sensitive investment selection—they create a comprehensive framework for income tax optimization. The benefits ripple outward. Trust assets grow more rapidly, beneficiaries receive distributions with minimized tax drag, and the grantor's estate is gradually reduced without formal gifts. Families who embrace this level of planning transform tax compliance from a burdensome obligation into a lever for preserving and multiplying wealth.

Tax planning in grantor trusts thus exemplifies the broader principle of estate planning: foresight creates opportunity. Just as failing to plan exposes families to the inefficiencies of probate, failing to integrate income tax strategies into trust management forfeits one of the most powerful tools available for wealth preservation. The complexity of income taxation may indeed baffle even the most brilliant minds, but through deliberate planning, families can turn that complexity to their advantage, ensuring that their financial legacy is not consumed by taxes but fortified against them.

5.2 Estate Tax Integration and Valuation Strategies

Estate tax remains one of the most significant threats to the preservation of multigenerational wealth. While the federal exemption levels have fluctuated considerably over time depending on the political climate, the fundamental principle persists: wealth transferred beyond exemption thresholds may be subject to substantial taxation. For families whose estates surpass these limits, trust planning becomes not merely desirable but essential. Integrating estate tax considerations into trust funding requires a blend of technical precision and strategic foresight, with special attention to annual gifting opportunities, valuation discounts, and exemption utilization.

The simplest yet most effective tool in estate tax planning is the use of annual exclusion gifts. The Internal Revenue Code allows individuals to transfer a certain amount each year to as many beneficiaries as they choose, without consuming any of their lifetime exemption. When coordinated with trust funding, these gifts become even more powerful. To qualify, however, contributions must constitute a present interest in property, meaning the recipient must have immediate access or control. Trusts resolve this tension through mechanisms such as Crummey powers, which grant beneficiaries a temporary right to withdraw contributions. While beneficiaries rarely exercise this right, its existence satisfies the present interest requirement, ensuring that gifts qualify for the exclusion. In situations where contributions exceed the annual limit, planners may employ so-called hanging powers, which defer the exercise of withdrawal rights into future years, maximizing the use of annual exclusions without triggering gift tax. Families with multiple beneficiaries can multiply these advantages, coordinating gifts across several trusts and generations, thereby shifting substantial wealth over time in a tax-efficient manner.

Beyond annual exclusions, valuation discounts provide another critical lever for reducing estate tax exposure. When transferring business interests, families can often apply minority interest discounts, reflecting the reduced value of non-controlling stakes, as well as marketability discounts, recognizing the difficulty of selling closely held interests. These discounts, when properly substantiated, can reduce the taxable value of transfers by as much as 30 to 40 percent. Appraisal rigor is paramount, as the Internal Revenue Service closely scrutinizes discount claims. Independent, defensible valuations not only withstand audit but also provide clarity for both trustees and beneficiaries.

Real estate presents its own valuation complexities. While the fair market value of property is generally determined by appraisal, strategic considerations can influence timing and method. Depressed market conditions may offer opportunities to transfer property at lower valuations, locking in tax benefits before recovery. Fractional interest transfers can also justify discounts, particularly when property is co-owned by multiple family members, as the lack of unilateral control diminishes market value. Similarly, life insurance policies require careful valuation when transferred into trusts. While the replacement cost or interpolated terminal reserve value often governs, subtle differences in policy structure can significantly affect taxable value. By understanding and applying these nuances, families maximize the leverage of transfers while minimizing tax exposure.

At the core of estate tax planning lies the lifetime exemption, a powerful but finite resource. Strategic allocation of this exemption ensures that it delivers maximum benefit. For example, transferring appreciating assets early in life removes both the initial value and subsequent growth from the taxable estate, magnifying the impact of exemption usage. Coordinating lifetime exemption use with generation-skipping transfer (GST) exemption amplifies these benefits, enabling assets to bypass intermediate layers of taxation as they pass to grandchildren or more remote descendants. The synergy between estate and GST exemptions is particularly potent in dynasty trusts, which can compound wealth across multiple generations free from repeated taxation.

Married couples face additional opportunities through portability, which allows a surviving spouse to claim the unused exemption of the deceased spouse. While portability offers flexibility, it requires careful timing and filing of the estate tax return, even when no tax is due. Couples who neglect this step risk losing millions of dollars in available exemptions. Coordinating portability with trust planning ensures that both spouses' exemptions are fully utilized while preserving flexibility for survivor needs. This combination of gifting, valuation discounts, and exemption planning forms the bedrock of estate tax efficiency, transforming complex rules into strategies that secure wealth for future generations.

5.3 State Tax Considerations and Multi-Jurisdictional Planning

While federal estate tax planning often dominates attention, state-level taxation can be equally impactful, particularly for families with multi-jurisdictional ties. States vary dramatically in their treatment of both income and estate taxation, creating a patchwork landscape that demands strategic navigation. Trust situs, residency planning, and international compliance all play pivotal roles in ensuring that trusts operate efficiently across borders.

One of the most powerful tools in this context is the deliberate selection of trust situs. Because trusts are creatures of state law, the jurisdiction chosen for administration determines not only legal interpretation but also state income tax liability. States such as Nevada, South Dakota, and Delaware offer highly favorable regimes, including the absence of state income tax, strong asset protection statutes, and extended perpetuities periods. Relocating trust situs to one of these jurisdictions can dramatically reduce or eliminate state income tax burdens, particularly for large trusts with significant investment income. Remote administration capabilities and modern technology now make it possible for families to select situs independent of physical residence, further expanding opportunities.

However, situs selection must be coordinated with state-specific rules such as the throwback tax, which some jurisdictions impose on accumulated trust income distributed to beneficiaries later. These rules can undermine deferral strategies by taxing income retroactively when it finally reaches beneficiaries. Careful planning ensures that distributions are timed and structured to minimize or avoid such penalties, aligning trust administration with both federal and state rules. For families with beneficiaries in multiple states, apportionment becomes another challenge. Income must often be allocated across states based on residency or source, creating potential for double taxation if not carefully managed. Trustees must therefore understand not only the situs rules of the trust but also the tax regimes of each beneficiary's state of residence.

State estate taxes add another layer of complexity. While the federal exemption has risen substantially in recent decades, many states maintain far lower thresholds, exposing estates to taxation even when no federal liability exists. Residency and domicile become critical planning tools in this context. Families with ties to multiple states may intentionally establish domicile in jurisdictions without estate taxes, ensuring that their estates avoid unnecessary levies. This may involve not only physical relocation but also legal steps such as registering to vote, obtaining driver's licenses, and filing state tax returns. For those unwilling or unable to relocate, optimization of state-specific exemptions and deductions becomes vital, requiring coordination with local statutes.

Trust migration offers yet another avenue for minimizing state estate taxes. By moving an existing trust from a high-tax jurisdiction to one with more favorable rules, families can achieve significant savings while preserving continuity. Migration may involve decanting into a new trust or modifying governing law provisions, both of which require careful compliance with statutory requirements. The decision to migrate must weigh potential tax savings against administrative complexity and beneficiary expectations, ensuring that the process strengthens rather than destabilizes governance.

International considerations compound these challenges for families with global assets or beneficiaries. U.S. persons with interests in foreign trusts face extensive reporting obligations, including Form 3520 and Form 3520-A. Failure to comply carries severe penalties, underscoring the need for rigorous compliance frameworks. Transfer pricing rules further complicate matters for international family businesses, requiring that intercompany transactions reflect arm's-length principles to avoid tax penalties. For families with multinational operations, aligning trust structures with transfer pricing compliance ensures both tax efficiency and regulatory integrity.

Tax treaties provide another layer of planning opportunity. Bilateral treaties between the United States and other nations often reduce or eliminate double taxation, clarify residency rules, and provide mechanisms for resolving disputes. By strategically aligning trust structures with treaty provisions, families can optimize cross-border wealth transfers, ensuring that income and estate taxation are minimized across jurisdictions. This requires not only legal expertise but also a global perspective, recognizing that wealth today rarely respects national boundaries.

State and international tax planning thus underscores the central truth of modern estate planning: jurisdiction matters as much as strategy. Families that proactively manage situs, domicile, and compliance transform a potential minefield into a landscape of opportunity. By integrating state and international considerations into their planning frameworks, they ensure that trusts operate not only within the letter of the law but also at the highest level of efficiency, preserving wealth across both borders and generations.

Chapter 6: Beneficiary Rights, Distributions, and Conflict Resolution

"The measure of a man is what he does with power." — Plato

Wealth, when placed within a trust, is not an end in itself but a means of providing for the next generation and ensuring continuity of values, stability, and opportunity. Yet history and statistics reveal the fragility of this endeavor. Research consistently shows that 65% of family wealth disappears by the second generation, and by the third generation, nearly 90% has vanished. While market volatility and taxation contribute to these losses, the most significant culprits are poor communication, unprepared heirs, and ill-defined distribution frameworks. A trust that fails to articulate how and why distributions should occur risks undermining the very purpose for which it was created. For this reason, developing and implementing a coherent distribution philosophy is not merely a technical necessity but a moral imperative. It represents the intersection of fiduciary responsibility, family culture, and long-term vision.

6.1 Distribution Philosophy Development and Implementation

The philosophy underlying trust distributions shapes the relationship between trustees and beneficiaries as much as the assets themselves. Trustees must balance fairness with prudence, generosity with sustainability, and flexibility with discipline.

When the guiding principles of distribution are thoughtfully designed and clearly expressed, they reduce ambiguity, prevent conflict, and align financial resources with family values.

One approach that has gained prominence is the design of incentive trusts, which link distributions to specific achievements or behaviors. By tying wealth transfers to educational milestones, trusts encourage beneficiaries to pursue higher learning, complete degrees, or engage in professional training. Career development incentives further extend this philosophy, rewarding sustained employment, entrepreneurial initiative, or professional certifications. The goal is not to dictate choices but to align distributions with personal growth, ensuring that wealth serves as a motivator rather than a substitute for effort.

Philanthropic participation requirements introduce another dimension. Some families choose to condition distributions on volunteerism, charitable giving, or participation in community projects. These provisions reinforce a culture of service, embedding the idea that wealth carries responsibilities beyond personal consumption. By weaving philanthropy into the trust's fabric, families transmit values alongside financial capital, ensuring that heirs see themselves as stewards rather than mere recipients.

Trusts can also address sensitive issues such as substance abuse by incorporating support mechanisms into distribution frameworks. Instead of enabling destructive behavior, trusts may provide for treatment, counseling, or rehabilitation as a condition for continued support. This approach recognizes the trustee's dual role as both guardian of wealth and protector of beneficiaries' well-being. By embedding compassion and accountability into the trust's philosophy, families confront challenges openly rather than leaving them to chance.

Distribution strategies must also account for the progression of life stages. Age-based schedules remain one of the most common frameworks, releasing portions of principal at predetermined ages, such as twenty-five, thirty, and thirty-five. These benchmarks aim to balance access with maturity, ensuring that beneficiaries are not overwhelmed by sudden wealth at a young age. Yet rigid age thresholds can fail to account for individual circumstances, leading some families to prefer hybrid models that combine age-based access with trustee discretion.

Emergencies, by their nature, defy schedules. A well-designed trust anticipates the unpredictable, authorizing distributions for unexpected circumstances such as medical crises, job loss, or natural disasters. Establishing protocols for emergency distributions ensures that help is available when truly needed, without opening the door to frivolous claims. Trustees tasked with administering these provisions must apply judgment carefully, documenting decisions to preserve both fairness and transparency.

Health and education expenses often receive priority in distribution frameworks. These categories represent investments in beneficiaries' human capital and long-term well-being, rather than mere consumption. By prioritizing tuition, healthcare, and related expenses, trusts align distributions with the grantor's vision of empowerment. Beneficiaries are supported in ways that enhance their independence and resilience, rather than being shielded from life's responsibilities.

Discretionary distribution guidelines further shape how trustees balance competing needs. Some trusts grant broad authority, empowering trustees with absolute discretion to determine when and how to distribute funds. Others adopt a "best interest" standard, requiring trustees to consider the beneficiary's welfare without surrendering to every request. The tension between discretion and entitlement is central to trust administration. Too much rigidity risks alienating beneficiaries, while too much leniency can deplete assets prematurely.

Trustees navigating these choices benefit from structured needs assessments and documentation. By requiring beneficiaries to submit requests in writing, accompanied by explanations of purpose and need, trustees create a record that supports consistent decision-making. This process not only protects the trustee legally but also encourages beneficiaries to reflect on their requests, fostering financial discipline.

For complex distribution decisions, external advisors often play a role. Trustees may consult financial planners, attorneys, or therapists to evaluate requests that touch on specialized knowledge or sensitive circumstances. For example, determining whether a business venture merits funding requires investment expertise, while approving support for rehabilitation may demand input from medical professionals. Incorporating external advisors ensures that decisions are informed, balanced, and defensible, reinforcing both fairness and fiduciary prudence.

At the heart of distribution philosophy lies a paradox: wealth is both a gift and a potential burden. Without guidance, it risks eroding motivation, fueling conflict, or fostering dependence. With thoughtful design, however, it becomes a tool for empowerment, resilience, and shared purpose. Incentive structures, life-stage frameworks, discretionary standards, and advisory mechanisms all converge to transform distributions from transactions into instruments of legacy.

Implementing such a philosophy requires ongoing commitment. Trustees must not only follow provisions mechanically but interpret them in ways that reflect both the letter and spirit of the trust. Regular communication with beneficiaries fosters understanding, reduces resentment, and builds trust in the governance process. By articulating the rationale behind distributions, trustees shift the narrative from arbitrary decisions to principled stewardship. Beneficiaries who understand the "why" behind distributions are more likely to accept limitations, respect the process, and view the trust as a partner in their lives rather than a distant authority.

Ultimately, distribution philosophy is where the technical and the human converge. It is where tax law, fiduciary duty, and financial management intersect with values, relationships, and aspirations. Crafting and implementing this philosophy is not about rigid formulas but about cultivating a framework that is resilient enough to withstand legal scrutiny, flexible enough to adapt to unforeseen circumstances, and human enough to reflect the family's identity. In doing so, families confront the sobering statistics of wealth dissipation and rewrite the narrative, transforming trusts from fragile vessels into enduring legacies.

6.2 Communication Protocols and Transparency Initiatives

If the history of family wealth dissipation teaches anything, it is that silence and secrecy are corrosive forces. The erosion of wealth across generations is rarely the result of market misfortune alone; more often it stems from misaligned expectations, lack of clarity, and a breakdown of trust in both senses of the word. Communication protocols and transparency initiatives form the scaffolding that prevents these fractures, ensuring that beneficiaries are not merely passive recipients of funds but active participants in a shared legacy. By embedding structures for regular dialogue, clear disclosure, and proactive conflict prevention, trusts evolve from static instruments into living institutions that adapt to family dynamics while preserving harmony.

The foundation of effective communication often lies in establishing structured family meetings. These gatherings, held annually or more frequently as circumstances dictate, create space for trustees to report on the trust's activities, investment performance, and strategic direction. Annual reports should not be dry compilations of numbers but educational tools that foster financial literacy among beneficiaries. Trustees who take the time to explain balance sheets, income statements, and investment returns in accessible language empower beneficiaries to understand not just what the trust contains, but how it functions. Involving the next generation in these meetings ensures that they grow up with familiarity and comfort around the responsibilities of wealth. Rather than encountering trust documents as impenetrable legal jargon in adulthood, they learn early how governance decisions are made and what values underlie them.

For families with complex dynamics or histories of conflict, professional facilitators can play an invaluable role. Neutral experts in wealth psychology or family governance can guide discussions, manage difficult conversations, and ensure that all voices are heard. By reducing the risk of meetings devolving into disputes, facilitators create an environment where transparency strengthens relationships rather than exacerbating tensions. Over time, these meetings can evolve into family forums where trust business is integrated with broader discussions of values, philanthropy, and long-term vision.

Transparency also requires clear standards for information disclosure. Beneficiaries cannot develop confidence in trustees or the trust itself if they are kept in the dark. Access to trust documents is the starting point, coupled with explanations of key terms and provisions in plain language. Legalistic opacity serves only to alienate beneficiaries, fostering suspicion and resentment. By contrast, open access and clear explanations build alignment between trustee intent and beneficiary expectations.

Investment performance reporting and fee disclosure are equally critical. Beneficiaries deserve to know not only the returns generated but also the costs incurred. Transparent reporting ensures that trustees are accountable, discouraging excessive fees or imprudent strategies. Similarly, distribution decisions should not appear arbitrary. When trustees explain the reasoning behind approvals or denials, including references to trust provisions or long-term sustainability, they transform what might otherwise feel like personal judgments into principled decisions.

Establishing appeal processes, whether through advisory committees or external mediators, further reinforces fairness and prevents small disputes from escalating into entrenched conflicts.

Conflict prevention strategies extend beyond reporting to the realm of shared purpose. Families that articulate mission statements and clarify their values create a compass that guides both trustees and beneficiaries. A mission statement might emphasize education, entrepreneurship, philanthropy, or intergenerational support, providing a framework that transcends individual disagreements. When distributions or investment decisions are viewed through the lens of these shared values, they gain legitimacy and reduce opportunities for conflict.

Integrating mediation or arbitration clauses into trust documents provides a formal mechanism for resolving disputes without resorting to costly and public litigation. These clauses demonstrate foresight, acknowledging that conflicts are inevitable but ensuring they are addressed constructively. Professional family counseling and wealth psychology services provide another dimension, addressing the emotional undercurrents that often drive disputes. By treating conflict as both a legal and psychological phenomenon, families strengthen resilience and cohesion.

In essence, communication protocols and transparency initiatives create a culture of openness, accountability, and shared responsibility. They transform trusts from opaque structures that breed resentment into transparent frameworks that foster understanding. Families who embrace these practices not only preserve wealth but also preserve relationships, ensuring that the legacy they pass forward is one of unity rather than division.

6.3 Advanced Beneficiary Empowerment Strategies

While transparency and communication ensure that beneficiaries understand their roles, true resilience requires more: empowerment. Trusts that merely distribute funds risk creating dependency, but trusts that actively cultivate leadership, entrepreneurship, and purpose transform wealth into a catalyst for growth. Advanced strategies for beneficiary empowerment move beyond compliance and into the realm of legacy, equipping heirs with the skills, values, and opportunities to steward wealth responsibly.

Next-generation leadership development is one avenue for empowerment. Families increasingly use trusts to support education not only in traditional academic fields but also in governance and civic engagement. Beneficiaries may be prepared for service on boards of nonprofits or family foundations, gaining experience in decision-making, oversight, and accountability. This training not only benefits the individual but also strengthens the family's philanthropic presence, embedding service as a core element of legacy. Similarly, entrepreneurial heirs may receive trust support for venture capital participation, provided such initiatives are vetted for feasibility and aligned with fiduciary standards. By supporting entrepreneurship, trusts encourage beneficiaries to create rather than merely consume, channeling wealth into innovation and productivity.

Impact investing education extends empowerment into the realm of values-based finance. Beneficiaries who understand how to align investments with social and environmental goals are better equipped to integrate wealth with purpose. Trusts can allocate portions of portfolios to sustainable enterprises, renewable energy, or community development projects, with beneficiaries actively involved in evaluating and monitoring impact. In this way, financial literacy is paired with ethical stewardship, ensuring that heirs see wealth as a tool for change rather than a passive inheritance.

Trust modification mechanisms provide another layer of empowerment. Trusts drafted decades ago may no longer reflect contemporary realities, and beneficiaries must have avenues for adaptation. Judicial modification remains one option, but non-judicial alternatives such as consent agreements or decanting have gained prominence. Virtual representation provisions ensure that the interests of minors or unborn descendants are protected, enabling families to modernize structures without disenfranchising vulnerable members. By participating in modification processes, beneficiaries experience governance as an evolving conversation rather than an unalterable decree, reinforcing their sense of agency.

Decanting powers, in particular, offer opportunities for modernization. Trustees with authority to "pour" assets into new trusts can adapt terms to reflect changes in tax law, family structure, or investment philosophy. When beneficiaries are consulted in these processes, they gain insight into the mechanics of governance and see firsthand how flexibility preserves relevance. This engagement fosters both transparency and trust, deepening the sense of partnership between trustees and beneficiaries.

Exit strategies and trust termination planning also play a role in empowerment. Trusts are not always intended to last forever, and circumstances may arise where early termination serves the family's best interests. By establishing clear triggers for early termination—such as asset levels falling below efficient thresholds or the satisfaction of primary objectives—families provide predictability. Beneficiaries may be given opportunities to buy out interests, ensuring fairness while preserving continuity. Tax minimization strategies, such as structuring distributions to avoid unnecessary gains, further enhance efficiency.

Post-termination planning is equally important. When a trust dissolves, families must coordinate to ensure that assets are distributed equitably and that the legacy it embodied does not dissolve with it. Family councils, mission statements, or successor structures such as foundations can carry forward the values that animated the trust. In this way, termination does not signify the end of stewardship but the transition into a new chapter.

Advanced empowerment strategies therefore complete the circle of trust governance. Transparency ensures understanding, education cultivates competence, and empowerment fosters agency. Together, these practices transform beneficiaries from passive heirs into active stewards. Families that embrace empowerment reduce the risks of wealth dissipation and increase the likelihood that their legacy will endure not only in financial terms but also in meaning and purpose.

Chapter 7: Digital Assets and Modern Trust Administration

"The best way to predict the future is to create it." — Peter Drucker

The trust, an institution born out of medieval necessity, finds itself at the center of one of the most profound transformations in wealth management since its inception. The rise of digital assets—cryptocurrencies, tokens, digital securities, and blockchain-based property rights—has introduced a new frontier for trustees, beneficiaries, and advisors. These assets, once the realm of speculative enthusiasts, now constitute a significant portion of modern portfolios. By 2025, estimates suggest that digital assets will represent between 15 and 25 percent of the average American's wealth. Yet, strikingly, only a small fraction of existing trusts—barely 12 percent—have provisions that directly address their management. This gap between reality and preparation signals both risk and opportunity. If trusts fail to adapt, they risk obsolescence; if they succeed, they ensure that digital wealth is not only preserved but integrated into broader legacies with the same care once afforded to land, businesses, and securities.

7.1 Cryptocurrency and Digital Currency Integration

Cryptocurrencies and other blockchain-based assets pose both promise and peril for trust administration. Their decentralized nature defies traditional models of custody and oversight, while their volatility and regulatory uncertainty complicate valuation, reporting, and distribution. For trustees, the challenge is not merely technical but philosophical: how to incorporate assets designed to bypass intermediaries into structures that rely on fiduciary governance. Meeting this challenge requires robust security protocols, clear tax strategies, and ongoing compliance with evolving regulatory frameworks.

The first and most urgent concern is custody. Unlike traditional securities, digital assets are secured through cryptographic keys, which function as both proof of ownership and access mechanism. Losing a private key means irrevocably losing the asset; no court, bank, or authority can restore it. Trustees, therefore, must implement advanced custody arrangements to prevent loss, theft, or unauthorized use. Multi-signature wallets offer one solution. By requiring multiple parties to approve a transaction, they reduce the risk of unilateral misuse and create accountability structures that mirror fiduciary checks and balances. For instance, a wallet might require the joint authorization of both a trustee and a professional custodian before funds can move, ensuring both oversight and security.

Deciding between hot wallets and cold storage adds another dimension. Hot wallets, connected to the internet, provide speed and accessibility but expose assets to hacking risks. Cold storage, by contrast, involves offline devices or even physical hardware secured in vaults, offering far greater protection at the cost of convenience. Trustees must balance liquidity needs with security imperatives, often using tiered strategies where a small portion remains in hot wallets for operational purposes while the bulk resides in cold storage. As digital assets rise in value and significance, trustees increasingly consider insurance coverage as well. Specialized policies now exist to protect against theft, hacking, or custodian insolvency, creating a risk mitigation framework that aligns digital custody with the standards expected of traditional financial assets.

Tax implications further complicate integration. Unlike traditional currencies, cryptocurrencies are treated as property by the Internal Revenue Service. Each transaction—whether a purchase, exchange, or even a simple transfer—may trigger taxable events requiring detailed basis calculations. Trustees must implement rigorous tracking systems to record acquisition costs, holding periods, and disposal proceeds. Failure to do so risks not only underpayment of taxes but also exposure to penalties for inaccurate reporting.

New dimensions of taxation have also emerged with the rise of staking and mining. Trustees managing digital assets must recognize that rewards earned through staking—where tokens are locked to validate transactions and earn new coins—are treated as taxable income, even if no liquidity event occurs. Similarly, mining income, derived from solving computational puzzles, creates taxable obligations based on fair market value at the time of receipt. These complexities demand integration of specialized accounting software and, often, collaboration with tax advisors versed in blockchain. For trusts with beneficiaries or transactions spanning borders, international compliance adds yet another layer. Transfers between wallets across jurisdictions may trigger reporting under regimes such as the Foreign Account Tax Compliance Act (FATCA) or equivalent foreign disclosure rules. Trustees cannot afford to treat these assets as invisible simply because they exist on decentralized ledgers; transparency is both a fiduciary and legal obligation.

The regulatory landscape remains fluid, and trustees must navigate it with vigilance. The Securities and Exchange Commission (SEC) continues to refine its stance on digital securities, clarifying when tokens qualify as investment contracts subject to securities law. Trustees who fail to recognize these classifications risk inadvertent violations, particularly when dealing with newer tokenized assets. Similarly, trust companies that provide advisory or investment services related to digital assets must comply with investment advisor regulations, including fiduciary standards and disclosure requirements. Anti-money laundering (AML) laws further apply, obligating trustees to implement know-your-customer (KYC) protocols when managing cryptocurrency transactions. Given the pseudonymous nature of blockchain, these requirements demand careful verification to ensure that trust assets are not tainted by illicit activity.

State-level trust laws are also evolving to recognize digital assets explicitly. Jurisdictions such as Delaware and Wyoming have enacted statutes clarifying that fiduciaries may custody, manage, and even delegate responsibility for digital assets under defined frameworks. These statutes provide trustees with legal certainty, reducing the risk of liability for prudent management. At the same time, the rapid pace of innovation means that trustees must continually update policies to reflect legislative change. What is permissible in one jurisdiction may remain uncertain in another, requiring multi-jurisdictional trusts to maintain agility and vigilance.

Integration of cryptocurrency into trusts thus requires more than mechanical transfer. It demands the creation of governance systems that respect both the technical realities of blockchain and the fiduciary obligations of trustees. Security protocols such as multi-signature wallets and cold storage preserve access, while insurance mitigates risks. Tax reporting frameworks ensure compliance with evolving interpretations of property law and income recognition. Regulatory adherence, from SEC guidance to AML compliance, embeds legitimacy. Together, these strategies transform what might otherwise appear as unruly, speculative assets into legitimate components of a family's estate plan.

Yet the true test lies not only in technical competence but also in vision. Trustees must recognize that digital assets are not a passing fad but a structural feature of modern wealth. Their integration into trusts signals an acknowledgment that stewardship must evolve with society. Just as trustees once adapted to railroads, industrial enterprises, and global securities markets, they must now adapt to decentralized finance and blockchain economies. The challenge is profound, but so too is the opportunity: to create trusts that are not relics of the past but engines of the future, capable of carrying wealth—and values—into a digital age.

7.2 Digital Identity and Online Asset Management

The rise of digital life has created a parallel reality in which identity, reputation, and value extend far beyond the physical. For trustees, the responsibility of managing estates now encompasses not only tangible wealth and financial portfolios but also the constellation of online accounts, intellectual property, and digital presence that collectively form a modern legacy. These assets, while intangible, can hold extraordinary financial and sentimental value. They require thoughtful integration into trust administration, ensuring that the digital footprints of individuals are preserved, transferred, or retired in ways consistent with their wishes.

A particularly pressing area involves social media and digital content rights. For creators—whether influencers, writers, artists, or entrepreneurs—social media accounts can represent lucrative intellectual property, generating ongoing advertising revenues, licensing deals, or subscription income. Even outside the realm of professional creators, personal accounts carry deep meaning for families, serving as archives of memories, relationships, and milestones. Trusts must address the succession of these accounts explicitly, designating who will assume control, how accounts will be managed, and whether they will continue, be memorialized, or be deleted. Platforms like Facebook and Instagram have begun offering memorial management tools, but without clear trust provisions, disputes can arise over access and control. Intellectual property generated through online channels—such as YouTube videos, podcasts, or e-books— requires careful treatment as monetizable assets. Trustees may be tasked with managing contracts, continuing licensing arrangements, or overseeing royalties, ensuring that digital creations remain sources of income rather than being lost in neglect.

Digital reputation management adds yet another layer. In an era where a single post can shape perception, the stewardship of online identity is a matter of both dignity and strategy. Trustees must ensure that the deceased's online presence is preserved respectfully and that personal brands or professional reputations are not misused. Reputation can be as valuable as property, influencing family businesses, philanthropic initiatives, or public legacies. By proactively planning for digital identity, families avoid situations where social media accounts are hijacked, neglected, or exploited, preserving both legacy and integrity.

Technology platforms themselves present unique challenges for access management. Unlike traditional bank accounts, online platforms often restrict transfers of ownership or forbid password sharing under their terms of service. This raises practical issues for trustees tasked with managing digital estates. Password management systems, combined with two-factor authentication protocols, have become essential. Families must decide how credentials will be stored, accessed, and updated, ensuring that trustees can fulfill their duties without breaching legal agreements or compromising security. Cloud storage—often containing invaluable documents, photographs, and creative works—presents similar considerations. Ownership and access rights must be clearly documented to avoid loss or disputes. Subscription-based services, ranging from software licenses to streaming platforms, also require attention. Trustees must identify which subscriptions should be terminated to prevent waste, which licenses may be transferred, and how ongoing obligations are to be managed.

Digital business assets elevate the stakes further. For many entrepreneurs, the heart of their business is no longer a storefront or factory but an online platform. E-commerce stores hosted on platforms like Shopify, Amazon, or Etsy often generate substantial revenue streams. Trustees must ensure continuity by maintaining ownership of accounts, preserving customer data, and overseeing operational processes. Failure to transfer access properly can result in the collapse of businesses that could otherwise sustain beneficiaries for years. Domain names represent another critical digital asset. A single domain may be worth millions, yet families frequently lose them to expiration due to neglect. Trust provisions must address not only ownership but also renewal strategies, ensuring that valuable domains remain secured.

Digital marketing assets—ranging from brand identities and customer lists to search engine rankings and advertising accounts—form the lifeblood of modern enterprises. Protecting and transferring these assets requires a blend of legal and technical expertise, ensuring that intellectual property rights are preserved, contracts are honored, and beneficiaries inherit not just tangible profits but the underlying engines of digital enterprise. In this sense, digital identity and online asset management extend far beyond personal convenience; they are core elements of legacy preservation in the twenty-first century.

7.3   Technology-Enhanced   Trust Administration

As trustees grapple with the complexities of digital identity and online assets, technology itself offers tools to enhance trust administration. The integration of artificial intelligence, blockchain, and advanced cybersecurity measures is reshaping the landscape of fiduciary practice. These innovations do not replace human judgment but augment it, providing trustees with precision, efficiency, and foresight. In doing so, they transform trusts from static repositories into adaptive systems capable of thriving in a rapidly evolving digital world.

Artificial intelligence provides a suite of capabilities that revolutionize both investment management and administrative efficiency. AI-assisted investment platforms can analyze vast quantities of data, identifying trends and opportunities that might elude traditional managers. For trusts, this means portfolios can be rebalanced dynamically, aligning risk tolerance with beneficiary needs while responding in real time to market conditions. AI can also streamline administrative functions, automatically calculating distributable net income, generating beneficiary notifications, and flagging anomalies for trustee review. Beyond mechanics, predictive analytics provide insights into long-term trust performance, forecasting how current strategies may impact future sustainability. Trustees armed with such tools make more informed decisions, preserving wealth while reducing costs.

Blockchain technology, the backbone of cryptocurrency, also offers transformative applications for trust documentation and verification. Smart contracts—self-executing agreements coded on a blockchain—allow certain trust functions to operate automatically. For instance, distributions could be triggered by predefined conditions, such as a beneficiary reaching a certain age or completing an educational milestone, reducing administrative burdens and ensuring consistency. Blockchain's immutable ledger provides a tamper-proof audit trail, securing records of amendments, distributions, and trustee actions. This transparency reduces disputes and enhances accountability, as every transaction is preserved in a verifiable form. More experimental applications explore the integration of decentralized autonomous organizations (DAOs) with traditional trusts, blending collective decision-making with fiduciary oversight. While still in early stages, these developments suggest a future where governance is increasingly participatory, blending legal tradition with decentralized innovation.

Cybersecurity forms the bedrock of all these technological advances. Trusts hold not only financial assets but also sensitive personal information, making them prime targets for cyberattacks. Advanced encryption protocols safeguard data, ensuring that communications, records, and credentials remain secure. Regular security audits and vulnerability assessments provide ongoing protection, identifying weaknesses before they are exploited. Trustees must also develop incident response plans, detailing how breaches will be contained, reported, and remedied. Transparency in these processes reassures beneficiaries that their wealth and privacy are protected with the same diligence applied to physical assets.

Technology-enhanced trust administration thus reflects a broader evolution: the recognition that fiduciary responsibility in the digital era requires both human discernment and technological sophistication. Artificial intelligence brings foresight and efficiency, blockchain introduces transparency and automation, and cybersecurity ensures resilience. Together, these innovations empower trustees to meet the demands of a digital world while upholding timeless fiduciary principles. The result is not a replacement of tradition but its renewal, ensuring that trusts remain relevant, effective, and trustworthy in an age where wealth is increasingly measured not only in dollars or property but also in data, identity, and digital presence.

Chapter 8: International Trust Planning and Cross-Border Considerations

"In the modern world, the intelligent way to prepare for the future is to prepare for anything." — Richard Florida

Global wealth has never been more mobile, nor more complex. Families now hold significant assets across multiple jurisdictions, from real estate in one country to corporate shares in another, with investment portfolios diversified across continents and digital assets that transcend borders altogether. International families control an estimated $84 trillion in global wealth, and nearly half of these families maintain assets in at least three countries. This reality makes cross-border estate planning not a niche concern but a mainstream necessity. Traditional trust frameworks, designed for single-jurisdiction estates, often prove inadequate in addressing the intricate interplay of tax regimes, creditor laws, reporting obligations, and cultural expectations that shape modern global wealth. International trust planning therefore emerges as a discipline in its own right—one that blends legal sophistication, financial strategy, and cultural sensitivity.

8.1 Pre-Immigration Trust Planning Strategies

The decision to immigrate to the United States, whether for opportunity, family, or lifestyle, carries profound implications for wealth management. The U.S. tax system is among the most comprehensive in the world, subjecting residents and citizens to worldwide income and estate taxation. For high-net-worth individuals, this shift can dramatically alter financial outcomes if not addressed proactively. Pre-immigration trust planning offers a suite of strategies that enable individuals and families to transition into the U.S. tax system in a way that preserves wealth, mitigates exposure, and aligns global holdings with long-term goals.

A critical element of pre-immigration planning is the use of foreign grantor trusts. These structures allow non-U.S. persons to establish trusts before acquiring residency, securing tax benefits that would be unavailable after immigration. One of the most valuable opportunities is the step-up in basis for appreciated foreign assets. By transferring assets into a properly structured trust before becoming a U.S. tax resident, individuals can reset the tax basis, minimizing capital gains exposure on future dispositions. This simple yet powerful maneuver can save millions in taxes, particularly for families with substantial foreign real estate or business interests.

Income tax deferral strategies also play an essential role. Transition periods between non-residency and residency create windows where income generated abroad may not be fully taxable in the United States. Pre-immigration trusts can capture these opportunities, deferring recognition of income until after the transition, when it may be taxed more favorably or offset by other planning techniques. Coupled with this, the maximization of gift and estate tax exemptions prior to residency can secure additional benefits. Transfers made before U.S. residency are often outside the scope of U.S. gift and estate taxation, allowing individuals to allocate wealth to heirs or trusts without diminishing future exemptions. Once residency begins, such opportunities narrow considerably, making timing a decisive factor.

Asset protection is another pillar of pre-immigration trust strategy. Moving assets across borders often exposes them to unfamiliar legal systems and creditor environments. Offshore jurisdictions with robust asset protection laws—such as the Cook Islands and Nevis—offer trusts that insulate wealth from potential claims. These jurisdictions are renowned for their protective statutes, short statutes of limitations for creditor actions, and strong defenses against foreign judgments. Selecting the appropriate jurisdiction requires careful comparative analysis, balancing the strength of legal protections against political stability, administrative sophistication, and reputational considerations.

Duress clauses further enhance resilience by empowering trustees to suspend distributions or relocate assets in response to political instability, coercion, or litigation threats. Emergency trust modification procedures, embedded within governing documents, ensure that structures remain adaptable even under extreme circumstances. These protective measures underscore a central truth of cross-border planning: wealth must not only grow but survive in environments where legal and political risks may be unpredictable.

International business succession adds additional complexity. Many global families operate enterprises that span jurisdictions, with subsidiaries in multiple countries, cross-border supply chains, and global customer bases. Pre-immigration trusts can be integrated with multi-jurisdictional family limited partnerships, ensuring that ownership and control are consolidated in a tax-efficient and protective manner. Coordinating trust structures with international corporate reorganizations ensures continuity, avoiding double taxation or unnecessary disruption of operations.

Family offices provide a natural hub for integrating these strategies. By centralizing oversight of investments, legal compliance, and family governance, family offices can coordinate across borders, aligning trusts with business entities and philanthropic initiatives. Charitable giving, for instance, often requires careful navigation of tax rules in multiple jurisdictions. Cross-border philanthropic planning ensures that donations qualify for deductions where possible, while also aligning with local cultural norms and regulatory requirements. Trusts can serve as vehicles for such philanthropy, channeling resources into global initiatives while reinforcing the family's values.

Pre-immigration trust planning is therefore not a narrow exercise in tax avoidance but a holistic strategy for securing global wealth in transition. It requires attentiveness to timing, precision in legal structuring, and sensitivity to cultural and political environments. By addressing basis step-ups, deferrals, exemptions, asset protection, and business succession, families entering the U.S. system can preserve not only their wealth but also their freedom to direct it in accordance with their goals.

The challenge lies in the interplay of complexity and urgency. Immigration often occurs under tight timelines, leaving little room for careful planning once residency is established. Families who act early, however, reap the benefits of foresight, ensuring that their wealth is not eroded by avoidable taxation or left vulnerable to unforeseen risks. Pre-immigration trust planning thus embodies the broader principle articulated by Richard Florida: in preparing for the future, families must prepare for anything.

8.2 Tax Treaty Optimization and Compliance Management

Cross-border families inevitably confront the challenge of double taxation. Without proper planning, income earned in one jurisdiction may be taxed both at the source and again in the country of residence. Tax treaties form the backbone of international coordination, mitigating this exposure while ensuring that families comply with multiple legal regimes. Yet treaties are not mechanical guarantees of relief; they are complex agreements that demand both strategic use and careful adherence. Trustees who manage international trusts must therefore develop expertise in treaty optimization, foreign reporting obligations, and investment structuring to ensure that wealth moves efficiently across borders without attracting unnecessary taxation or penalties.

Double taxation avoidance begins with the application of foreign tax credits, which allow taxes paid in one jurisdiction to offset liabilities in another. While straightforward in theory, this process requires precision in practice. Each treaty contains unique provisions governing eligibility, calculation, and limitations. Trustees must ensure that income classifications match across jurisdictions—interest, dividends, royalties, and capital gains may each receive different treatment. Moreover, anti-abuse rules designed to prevent "treaty shopping" impose substance requirements. Families cannot simply route investments through jurisdictions with favorable treaties unless genuine business activity or residence exists there. Failure to demonstrate economic substance may invalidate treaty benefits, exposing trusts to full double taxation.

When disputes arise—such as conflicting interpretations of residency, source of income, or permanent establishment rules—mutual agreement procedures provide a mechanism for resolution. These procedures allow competent authorities from both jurisdictions to negotiate outcomes, but they are lengthy and require meticulous documentation. Trustees must be prepared to present comprehensive records of transactions, residency ties, and business activities to substantiate claims. Transfer pricing adds further complexity when trusts hold interests in multinational businesses. Transactions between related entities must be conducted at arm's-length, with careful documentation of valuations and justifications. Otherwise, tax authorities may reallocate income, creating unexpected liabilities and undermining treaty relief.

Compliance with reporting requirements is equally critical. U.S. beneficiaries of foreign trusts face some of the most stringent disclosure obligations in the world. Forms 3520 and 3520-A must be filed to report transfers, ownership, and distributions from foreign trusts. Penalties for failure are severe, often calculated as percentages of the unreported assets or distributions, and can quickly eclipse the value of the trust itself. FATCA (the Foreign Account Tax Compliance Act) adds another layer, requiring disclosure of foreign financial assets exceeding specified thresholds. FATCA also obligates foreign financial institutions to report accounts held by U.S. taxpayers, creating a global web of transparency that makes non-compliance increasingly untenable. Trustees who fail to coordinate FATCA reporting risk exposing beneficiaries to penalties and audits.

For families already out of compliance, voluntary disclosure programs provide a pathway to resolution. While such programs require payment of taxes and penalties, they generally shield taxpayers from harsher consequences, including criminal prosecution. Trustees must weigh the benefits of disclosure against the costs, recognizing that global information exchange agreements make continued secrecy unsustainable. The emphasis in modern trust administration has shifted decisively from concealment to transparency, with planning strategies designed not to evade taxes but to manage them efficiently within compliant frameworks.

Investment structuring across jurisdictions requires particular care. Passive foreign investment companies (PFICs) create punitive tax consequences for U.S. taxpayers, imposing interest charges and ordinary income treatment on gains unless elections are made. Trusts that hold foreign mutual funds or similar vehicles risk triggering these rules, undermining tax efficiency. Controlled foreign corporations (CFCs) introduce similar issues when trusts hold significant stakes in foreign businesses. Income may be attributed to U.S. beneficiaries even without distributions, eroding deferral advantages. Trustees must therefore design portfolios that avoid PFIC and CFC pitfalls, often favoring tax-transparent structures or funds specifically designed for cross-border investors.

Tax-efficient fund structures—such as master-feeder arrangements, treaty-compliant vehicles, or jurisdiction-specific investment funds—can mitigate these challenges. By carefully aligning structures with treaty provisions and U.S. anti-deferral rules, trustees create portfolios that maximize returns while minimizing unnecessary taxation. These strategies demonstrate that international trust planning is not about hiding wealth but about navigating a labyrinth of rules with clarity, compliance, and foresight. Properly executed, treaty optimization and reporting management transform complexity into opportunity, enabling families to sustain global wealth with confidence.

8.3 Multi-Generational International Family Governance

The financial complexities of global wealth are matched by the human complexities of families that span continents, cultures, and generations. Preserving wealth across borders requires more than technical structuring; it demands governance systems that integrate values, resolve disputes, and maintain cultural continuity. Without these frameworks, even the most carefully crafted trusts may fracture under the weight of miscommunication, conflicting expectations, or cultural divides. Multi-generational international family governance therefore becomes an essential complement to tax and legal strategies, ensuring that wealth is not only preserved but also meaningful and cohesive.

A cornerstone of governance is the development of family constitutions. These documents, while not legally binding in the same sense as trust instruments, articulate the values, principles, and objectives that guide family wealth. For international families, constitutions must bridge cultural differences, harmonizing traditions, religious beliefs, and social expectations. They often set forth language protocols to ensure inclusivity, recognizing that heirs may grow up speaking different languages across generations. They may also outline frameworks for communication, such as rotating family meetings across global locations or establishing translation support. International education programs further reinforce unity, exposing younger members to shared history and cultural experiences. Exchange programs, philanthropy projects, and collaborative initiatives create bonds that transcend geography, anchoring wealth in a sense of shared identity.

Dispute resolution mechanisms are equally critical. Cross-border families face unique challenges when conflicts arise, as differing jurisdictions may compete for authority. Integrating arbitration and mediation clauses into trust documents provides a neutral mechanism for resolving disputes privately, efficiently, and consistently. Choice-of-law provisions clarify which jurisdiction's rules will govern, reducing uncertainty and preventing forum shopping. Technology has expanded possibilities further, enabling virtual family governance through secure platforms. Families dispersed across continents can now convene digitally, vote on governance decisions, and participate in advisory councils without the need for constant travel. These digital mechanisms ensure continuity and engagement while accommodating global dispersion.

Legacy preservation extends beyond financial capital to cultural assets. International families often hold art collections, historical properties, or philanthropic commitments that embody their heritage. Trusts can coordinate the preservation of these assets, ensuring that art is cataloged, insured, and displayed according to family wishes, or that historical estates are maintained as symbols of identity. Philanthropy provides another vehicle for cultural continuity. International charitable foundations allow families to express shared values on a global stage, whether through education, healthcare, or cultural initiatives. These foundations not only preserve legacy but also unite diverse branches of the family around common causes, reinforcing cohesion across borders.

Family business succession presents some of the greatest challenges for global governance. Multinational enterprises must navigate varying legal regimes, labor laws, and cultural expectations. Succession planning must therefore integrate both business and family governance, ensuring that leadership transitions respect cultural contexts while maintaining global strategy. Trusts can coordinate ownership structures, voting rights, and management succession, preventing fragmentation of control across jurisdictions. When aligned with family constitutions and dispute resolution mechanisms, such structures preserve both business continuity and family unity.

Ultimately, multi-generational governance is about creating resilience. It recognizes that wealth alone cannot hold a family together; it is shared purpose, cultural identity, and trust in governance processes that sustain legacy. By integrating constitutions, dispute resolution, and legacy preservation into their structures, international families transform wealth from a fragile inheritance into a durable platform for connection and continuity. In doing so, they ensure that their influence extends not only across borders but also across time, carrying forward values as enduring as the wealth that supports them.

Chapter 9: Charitable Integration and Philanthropic Strategies

"No one has ever become poor by giving." — Anne Frank

Philanthropy has always been woven into the fabric of legacy. It represents more than generosity; it is a conscious choice to align wealth with purpose, to ensure that financial success translates into enduring social value. In modern estate planning, charitable integration has taken on an increasingly strategic dimension. Families recognize that philanthropy is not only a moral calling but also a sophisticated tool for reducing tax burdens, strengthening family unity, and creating legacies that endure beyond material inheritance. Data confirms its potency: charitable giving through trust structures can reduce effective tax rates by 15 to 40 percent, all while enabling families to see their wealth generate tangible impact across multiple generations.

Charitable trusts occupy a special place within this framework. They provide a structured mechanism to balance income generation for beneficiaries with long-term commitments to causes that reflect family values. Among these, the charitable remainder trust (CRT) stands out as one of the most versatile and widely used vehicles, offering both tax benefits and opportunities for sustained giving. By blending income optimization with remainder gifts to charity, CRTs create a bridge between personal financial security and public good.

9.1 Charitable Remainder Trust Integration and Income Optimization

The integration of charitable remainder trusts into estate planning strategies requires careful attention to asset selection and timing. Not all assets are equally suited to CRT funding. Highly appreciated assets such as stocks, real estate, or business interests often represent the best candidates. Selling these assets outright would trigger significant capital gains taxes, eroding their value. By transferring them into a CRT, the grantor can avoid immediate recognition of gain, while the trust itself, as a tax-exempt entity, may sell the assets without incurring tax. This preserves the full value of the contribution, which can then be reinvested to generate income. Timing is critical as well. Funding a CRT during high-income years allows donors to benefit from substantial charitable deductions, offsetting tax liabilities while securing future income streams.

Income stream optimization is another critical dimension. CRTs require that a percentage of the trust's assets be paid out annually to the grantor or designated beneficiaries. Selecting the right payout rate balances immediate income needs with long-term growth of the remainder. A higher payout provides larger short-term distributions but diminishes the eventual charitable gift, while a lower payout preserves more for charity and future growth. Grantors must therefore weigh personal financial security against philanthropic goals. The "flip CRUT" strategy provides added flexibility, allowing the trust to begin as a net-income-only trust—distributing only what it actually earns—and later convert to a standard annuity payout. This approach is particularly useful when funding the trust with illiquid or non-income-producing assets such as real estate, which may take time to sell or generate consistent returns. Once liquidated, the trust "flips" to provide predictable income, ensuring both growth and stability.

Investment management within CRTs requires a delicate balance. Because CRTs are tax-exempt, trustees are free to pursue total return strategies without concern for generating taxable income. This allows for a broader, more growth-oriented approach, combining equities, bonds, and alternative investments. Some families may prioritize income-focused strategies, favoring dividend-paying stocks or fixed-income securities to ensure steady distributions. Others may adopt total return approaches, focusing on overall portfolio appreciation to sustain both income payments and remainder growth. Trustees must tailor strategies to the grantor's income needs, risk tolerance, and philanthropic aspirations.

Alternative investments can further enhance returns, though they carry risks that must be carefully managed. Private equity, hedge funds, or real estate funds may provide diversification and growth potential, but they require due diligence and liquidity management. A CRT, with its long-term horizon, can absorb certain illiquid investments, provided they align with payout obligations and overall risk profiles. Effective risk management becomes paramount, as overexposure to volatile assets could jeopardize both income distributions and charitable remainders. Diversification across asset classes, geographies, and industries ensures sustainability, preserving the CRT's ability to fulfill its dual mission of income generation and philanthropy.

The charitable remainder trust also introduces questions of coordination with heirs. Because the CRT ultimately directs its remainder to charity, heirs may receive less than they otherwise would through direct inheritance. Wealth replacement strategies provide solutions to this dilemma. One common approach involves life insurance trusts. By using a portion of CRT income to fund premiums on life insurance held within an irrevocable trust, families can replace the wealth directed to charity, ensuring that heirs are not disadvantaged. The result is a balance: the family supports philanthropy while also preserving inheritance for future generations.

Charitable lead trusts (CLTs) provide complementary strategies. Where CRTs prioritize income for beneficiaries and remainder gifts to charity, CLTs reverse the order, granting income streams to charities for a set period before transferring remainders to heirs. Combining CRTs and CLTs allows families to craft philanthropic plans that span multiple time horizons, serving both immediate charitable needs and long-term legacy goals. This dual approach creates resilience, enabling families to respond to changing financial circumstances or philanthropic opportunities while maintaining structural integrity.

Generation-skipping transfer tax planning intersects naturally with CRTs. By allocating GST exemptions strategically, families can ensure that CRT structures integrate smoothly into multi-generational planning. For instance, the remainder of a CRT may be directed to a charitable foundation that engages descendants in governance, blending philanthropy with education and leadership development. In this way, CRTs become not only tax-efficient vehicles but also instruments of cultural transmission, teaching heirs the responsibilities of stewardship.

What emerges from these strategies is a portrait of philanthropy as both pragmatic and principled. Charitable remainder trusts allow families to unlock the value of appreciated assets, generate income, secure tax benefits, and make meaningful charitable contributions. They embody the principle that financial planning is not merely about minimizing liabilities but about aligning wealth with values. In integrating CRTs into estate plans, families create legacies that are durable, flexible, and impactful—legacies that reduce tax burdens while uplifting communities.

The broader lesson is that giving, far from diminishing wealth, expands it in ways that transcend balance sheets. The tax benefits of CRTs are real and measurable, but their true value lies in their capacity to link personal prosperity with collective good. By weaving philanthropy into the fabric of estate planning, families ensure that their wealth does not merely pass forward but also reaches outward, touching lives beyond their own. In this sense, charitable integration through CRTs is not simply a financial tactic but a profound expression of legacy, one that fulfills Anne Frank's timeless observation: no one has ever become poor by giving.

9.2 Charitable Lead Trust Strategies for Transfer Tax Minimization

If the charitable remainder trust embodies the principle of giving later, the charitable lead trust (CLT) represents the philosophy of giving first. Unlike a CRT, which pays income to the donor or beneficiaries for a term before leaving the remainder to charity, a

CLT directs its initial income stream to charitable causes, with the remainder ultimately passing to heirs. This reversal of structure makes CLTs particularly powerful for minimizing transfer taxes while still preserving family wealth. By leveraging current valuations, interest rate environments, and tax benefits, CLTs enable families to create legacies that serve both charitable and familial objectives in a single elegant framework.

At the heart of CLT planning lies the distinction between grantor and non-grantor structures. A grantor CLT allows the donor to claim an immediate charitable income tax deduction based on the present value of the charitable lead interest. However, the donor must also include the trust's income on their personal return each year, effectively bearing the annual tax burden. For donors in high-income years, the front-loaded deduction can be enormously valuable, offsetting taxable income and reducing immediate liabilities. A non-grantor CLT, by contrast, does not provide an upfront deduction to the donor, but the trust itself is treated as a separate entity, claiming deductions for charitable payments and avoiding taxable income. The remainder interest eventually passes to heirs with significant gift and estate tax benefits, as the taxable value of the transfer is reduced by the actuarial value of the charitable payments. Families must weigh whether the immediate tax relief of the grantor CLT or the long-term estate planning benefits of the non-grantor CLT better aligns with their objectives.

Structural decisions further refine these strategies. Some CLTs are designed with reversionary interests, meaning that after the charitable term expires, assets return to the donor. Others provide for remainder beneficiaries, typically children or grandchildren, ensuring that wealth continues to flow within the family.

Reversionary designs maximize income tax deductions but may not create long-term wealth transfers, while remainder structures strike a balance between philanthropy and inheritance. The selection hinges on whether the donor's priority lies in immediate tax relief or in building intergenerational legacies.

The duration of the CLT is equally consequential. Term CLTs, which operate for a set number of years, rely heavily on actuarial calculations that determine the present value of charitable payments. The prevailing interest rate environment plays a decisive role: lower rates increase the value of charitable interests for tax purposes, reducing the taxable value of remainder transfers to heirs. Conversely, higher rates favor remainder beneficiaries, as the present value of charitable interests shrinks. Lifetime CLTs, which operate for the duration of the donor's life, add another dimension. They provide sustained charitable funding and long-term planning stability, but they introduce uncertainty in valuation due to lifespan variability. Families often integrate CLTs with family foundations, creating structures where annual payments fuel ongoing charitable initiatives that reinforce family values. Such integration transforms the CLT from a tax strategy into a vehicle for perpetual philanthropic identity.

Asset growth potential also influences outcomes. If assets within a CLT appreciate significantly during the charitable term, the excess growth passes to heirs with minimal transfer tax. Trustees therefore align investment strategies with both charitable payouts and long-term growth objectives, balancing current obligations with the preservation of remainder value. The result is a dual-purpose trust that maximizes impact across both fronts.

International charitable planning complicates matters further. U.S. tax law generally limits deductions to gifts made to qualified domestic charities, meaning that contributions to foreign organizations may not qualify unless equivalency determinations or specific certifications are secured. Families with global ties often face the challenge of aligning philanthropic intentions with tax realities. Equivalency determinations, which confirm that a foreign charity meets U.S. standards, enable deductions while maintaining international reach. For families wishing to establish philanthropic initiatives abroad, multi-jurisdictional family foundations may be required. These structures allow coordinated giving across borders while navigating the patchwork of legal and tax regimes that govern international philanthropy. Strategic planning ensures that generosity is not constrained by geography, allowing families to leave a truly global legacy.

Charitable lead trusts therefore embody a sophisticated intersection of tax planning, philanthropy, and family governance. By carefully selecting structures, terms, assets, and jurisdictions, families achieve immediate impact for charitable causes while ensuring that wealth transitions efficiently to heirs. In an era where both taxes and social expectations weigh heavily on wealthy families, CLTs offer a framework for aligning fiscal prudence with moral purpose.

9.3 Private Foundation Integration and Multi-Generational Governance

While charitable trusts provide flexible and efficient vehicles for giving, many families seek a more permanent and participatory structure for philanthropy. The private foundation has become a favored instrument for those who wish to formalize their charitable legacy, establish enduring institutions, and engage multiple generations in structured governance. By integrating private foundations with trusts and other vehicles, families create not only tax-efficient strategies but also platforms for education, leadership, and cultural transmission.

Establishing a family foundation begins with defining its operational framework. Board composition is central, often blending family members with independent directors who bring expertise in law, finance, or philanthropy. For multi-generational families, foundations serve as training grounds for younger heirs, preparing them for leadership roles by involving them in grantmaking, investment oversight, and governance. This process transforms wealth from a source of entitlement into a responsibility, cultivating skills and values that endure. Leadership development within the foundation becomes an act of legacy in itself, ensuring continuity of both charitable missions and family cohesion.

Grantmaking strategies define the impact of the foundation. Families may focus on education, healthcare, arts, or environmental causes, aligning philanthropic efforts with personal passions and values. Establishing clear frameworks for evaluating grant proposals, measuring outcomes, and ensuring accountability prevents mission drift and enhances effectiveness. Impact measurement, increasingly a standard in modern philanthropy, ensures that resources generate meaningful results rather than dissipating into inefficiency. Foundations that embrace transparency and accountability not only enhance their credibility but also model good governance for younger generations.

Administrative efficiency must also be considered. While private foundations offer control and permanence, they come with significant regulatory and reporting obligations. Families must manage operational costs carefully, ensuring that administrative burdens do not consume disproportionate resources. Trusts and donor-advised funds can be integrated to streamline operations, with foundations focusing on strategic leadership while other vehicles handle transactional giving.

Donor-advised funds (DAFs) have gained prominence as complementary tools. Unlike foundations, which require independent governance, DAFs allow donors to recommend grants while leaving administration to sponsoring organizations. Families often use DAFs to consolidate charitable contributions in high-income years, securing immediate tax deductions while distributing funds over time. Investment growth within DAFs further enhances giving potential, while simplified administration reduces complexity. Integrating DAFs with private foundations enables strategic flexibility: foundations provide governance and visibility, while DAFs offer efficiency and adaptability.

Philanthropy is increasingly shaped by impact investing and mission-related investment strategies. Families no longer see a strict divide between charitable giving and investment management. Program-related investments allow foundations to deploy capital in ways that generate both social impact and potential returns, such as low-interest loans to nonprofits or investments in community development projects. Environmental, social, and governance (ESG) integration aligns foundation portfolios with broader values, ensuring that investments do not contradict philanthropic missions. Some families adopt blended finance structures, combining philanthropic capital with private investment to magnify impact. These strategies transform philanthropy from a static exercise of grantmaking into a dynamic ecosystem where financial capital actively advances social goals.

The integration of private foundations, donor-advised funds, and impact investing illustrates the broader evolution of philanthropic governance. No longer limited to tax planning or symbolic giving, philanthropy has become a sophisticated arena for family engagement, leadership development, and cultural continuity. By institutionalizing generosity through foundations and complementing them with flexible vehicles, families ensure that their wealth does not dissipate into isolated acts of charity but flows through enduring structures that adapt to changing times.

Ultimately, private foundations embody the principle that philanthropy is not only about giving money but also about shaping legacy. They provide forums for family members to work together, learn governance, resolve differences, and translate values into action. In a world where wealth often fragments families, philanthropy becomes a unifying force, reminding them that prosperity carries obligations as well as privileges. By integrating foundations into trust and estate planning, families create legacies that span generations, blending tax efficiency with human purpose.

Chapter 10: Estate Planning Integration and Wealth Transfer Optimization

"An investment in knowledge pays the best interest." —
Benjamin Franklin

The true test of estate planning lies not in its technical perfection at the time of drafting but in its ability to carry wealth across generations with both efficiency and purpose. Families who rely solely on basic will-based planning often discover, too late, that a significant portion of their estates is lost to taxes, probate costs, and inefficiencies. By contrast, integrated estate planning that leverages properly structured revocable trusts and advanced transfer techniques can deliver between 25 and 35 percent more wealth to beneficiaries. This difference is not marginal; it is transformative, shaping whether family legacies endure or erode. At the heart of this efficiency lies a suite of strategies focused on the generation-skipping transfer (GST) tax and the creation of dynasty trusts—tools designed not merely to pass wealth forward but to ensure it endures for centuries.

10.1 Generation-Skipping Transfer Tax Planning and Dynasty Trust Strategies

The GST tax exists as a safeguard against perpetual avoidance of estate taxation. Without it, wealthy families could bypass children and transfer assets directly to grandchildren or great-grandchildren, avoiding multiple layers of taxation. The GST tax closes this loophole by imposing a separate levy on transfers that "skip" generations. Yet, like many aspects of tax law, the GST tax also creates opportunities for those who understand its intricacies. By allocating exemptions strategically and employing dynasty trusts, families can not only avoid repeated taxation but also establish structures that preserve and grow wealth indefinitely.

The first step in GST planning involves understanding allocation of exemptions. Each individual has a lifetime GST exemption, and its proper use determines how effectively assets can flow to future generations. A direct skip occurs when assets pass immediately to grandchildren or more remote descendants. An indirect skip, by contrast, involves transfers to trusts where beneficiaries may include multiple generations, but eventual distributions will bypass the children. The choice between direct and indirect strategies hinges on family structure, timing, and objectives. Trustees and planners must decide whether wealth should leap directly to grandchildren—perhaps to fund education or entrepreneurial ventures—or flow through flexible trusts that accommodate multiple generations.

Late allocation elections provide further flexibility. Families who fail to allocate GST exemptions at the time of transfer may make retroactive elections, often using formula clauses to ensure that allocations align with available exemptions and tax laws at the time of filing. These clauses, which adjust automatically to account for valuation changes or legislative shifts, protect families from errors that might otherwise create unintended liabilities. Precision in drafting is vital, as even minor missteps can disqualify exemptions or expose assets to unnecessary taxation.

Dynasty trusts represent the pinnacle of GST planning. Established in jurisdictions that allow perpetual or extended trust durations, dynasty trusts lock in GST exemptions for assets that can remain outside of taxable estates indefinitely. In states such as South Dakota, Nevada, or Delaware, trusts can last for hundreds of years—or, in some cases, perpetually—providing continuous support for descendants without repeated estate taxation. These trusts become more than legal tools; they are family institutions, preserving capital while distributing benefits in accordance with carefully crafted rules. By securing assets in dynasty trusts, families harness the power of compounding across multiple generations, creating a legacy that grows rather than diminishes with time.

Designing multi-generational trusts requires both flexibility and foresight. Distribution committees can be established to reflect changing family needs, blending representation from different branches of the family to ensure fairness. Such committees can decide on extraordinary distributions for education, healthcare, or entrepreneurial initiatives, allowing trusts to adapt to new circumstances without undermining long-term objectives. Trust protectors—individuals appointed with authority to modify terms or replace trustees—add another layer of adaptability. By granting powers to respond to legislative changes, family disputes, or unforeseen circumstances, trust protectors prevent rigidity from becoming a weakness.

Decanting and migration strategies extend this flexibility further. Decanting allows trustees to "pour" assets from one trust into a new one with improved terms, effectively modernizing outdated provisions. Migration permits relocation of trusts to more favorable jurisdictions, optimizing for tax laws, creditor protections, or administrative efficiency. Together, these strategies ensure that dynasty trusts remain resilient in the face of changing laws and evolving family dynamics.

Investment strategy forms the backbone of dynasty trust sustainability. Because these trusts are designed for perpetual or near-perpetual duration, they require growth-oriented allocations that can withstand the passage of time. Equity investments, with their potential for compounding, often form the core of such portfolios. Yet reliance on equities alone introduces volatility that could destabilize distributions. Alternative investments, including private equity, hedge funds, or infrastructure projects, provide diversification and potentially higher returns. Illiquid assets, such as closely held businesses or real estate, may also play a role, but trustees must balance their inclusion with liquidity needs for distributions.

Risk management becomes paramount when planning across centuries. A dynasty trust cannot be managed as though it were a single generational portfolio; it must span economic cycles, geopolitical shifts, and market revolutions. Diversification across asset classes, geographies, and industries protects against concentrated risks that could erode wealth. Trustees must also adapt investment strategies to the evolving needs of beneficiaries. For example, one generation may prioritize educational funding, while another may seek capital for entrepreneurship. Flexible yet disciplined investment governance ensures that trusts remain aligned with both fiduciary obligations and family aspirations.

The integration of dynasty trusts with GST planning highlights the profound leverage of foresight. By using exemptions wisely, employing formula clauses, and selecting jurisdictions that allow long-duration trusts, families can transform their estate plans into dynastic legacies. These structures ensure that wealth does not dissipate at each generational handoff but instead compounds, serving both immediate needs and long-term growth.

The efficiency gains are striking. Where traditional planning may see wealth reduced by taxes at each generational transfer, integrated GST and dynasty trust strategies preserve principal, enhance growth, and extend benefits for centuries. The difference between an estate plan that ends at the children's generation and one that endures across five or six generations is not merely quantitative but qualitative. It represents the difference between wealth as a fleeting inheritance and wealth as an enduring institution.

Ultimately, GST and dynasty trust strategies affirm the truth of Benjamin Franklin's observation: knowledge, when applied wisely, yields compounding benefits. Families who invest in understanding these tools, and who implement them with precision, create not only financial legacies but also institutional resilience. Their trusts stand as testaments to foresight, carrying wealth and values into futures their founders could scarcely imagine.

10.2 Business Succession Planning and Family Enterprise Continuity

For families whose wealth is intertwined with closely held businesses, estate planning cannot be separated from succession planning. A business is not merely an asset to be divided; it is often the heart of a family's identity, the source of livelihoods, and the embodiment of entrepreneurial vision. The transfer of such enterprises across generations requires not only legal and tax structuring but also cultural stewardship and preparation of future leaders. Trusts, when integrated with business succession frameworks, provide continuity, stability, and efficiency, ensuring that transitions occur smoothly rather than being mired in conflict or inefficiency.

Family limited partnerships (FLPs) remain one of the most powerful vehicles for combining estate planning with business succession. By consolidating ownership of business interests within an FLP, families achieve centralized management while retaining flexibility in transferring limited partnership interests to younger generations. The valuation discounts applied to minority and non-marketable interests can significantly reduce the taxable value of transfers, minimizing gift tax exposure. At the same time, the senior generation retains control through general partnership positions, gradually transitioning authority while mentoring successors. Trust integration magnifies these advantages, as limited partnership interests can be placed within irrevocable or dynasty trusts, protecting them from creditors and ensuring multi-generational continuity.

Management succession is not simply about legal ownership but about cultivating the capacity of the next generation. A carefully structured trust can require that heirs engage in training, complete education, or gain external professional experience before assuming leadership roles. This ensures that stewardship is grounded not in entitlement but in competence. Trusts can also appoint distribution committees or advisory boards composed of family members and independent advisors, striking a balance between legacy preservation and professional oversight. Such governance structures prepare heirs for both leadership and collaboration, reducing the risk of destructive disputes.

Buy-sell agreements provide the legal framework for smooth ownership transitions, particularly when businesses involve multiple shareholders or family branches. Coordinating these agreements with trust structures ensures that upon death, disability, or retirement of an owner, interests are transferred efficiently, funded by mechanisms such as life insurance or installment payments. Without such coordination, families risk liquidity crises, forced sales, or litigation. Trusts can hold ownership interests and serve as parties to buy-sell agreements, ensuring consistency and protecting against fragmentation. Exit strategy planning becomes equally important when families choose to sell businesses rather than perpetuate them. Here, trusts play a role in structuring proceeds to achieve tax efficiency while preserving capital for heirs.

Key employees often hold the balance of continuity during transitions. Incentivizing them ensures that the business survives leadership changes. Trusts can be used to establish management incentive plans, rewarding employees with equity or cash-based participation tied to performance metrics. Employee stock ownership plans (ESOPs) provide broader frameworks, enabling employees to acquire ownership over time, aligning their interests with the business's success. Trusts can coordinate with ESOP structures, holding shares on behalf of employees or integrating with other estate planning tools. Phantom equity and synthetic incentive plans, which provide cash-based rewards linked to business value without conferring actual ownership, offer flexible alternatives. Trusts managing these programs ensure that incentives are delivered consistently, reinforcing loyalty during periods of transition.

Exit strategy optimization requires both foresight and technical precision. Installment sales remain a common technique, allowing business owners to transfer interests while spreading tax liabilities over time. Trusts serve as vehicles for receiving installment payments, preserving liquidity and protecting assets. Seller financing, structured through trusts, ensures continuity of payments while protecting buyers and sellers alike. For owners who sell businesses outright, charitable remainder trusts can be coordinated to receive sale proceeds, deferring capital gains and providing income streams while ultimately benefiting philanthropy. Opportunity zone investments add another layer of tax optimization, allowing reinvestment of sale proceeds into designated areas with substantial deferral and exclusion benefits. By integrating these strategies into trust structures, families ensure that business exits do not merely trigger tax liabilities but open opportunities for growth, impact, and legacy preservation.

Ultimately, business succession planning is about balance: preserving the economic value of enterprises while honoring the relationships, values, and aspirations that built them. Trusts provide the scaffolding for that balance, ensuring that transitions are not moments of rupture but opportunities for continuity and renewal. Families who integrate succession planning with trust structures not only transfer wealth efficiently but also protect the integrity of the enterprises that define their legacy.

10.3 Advanced Wealth Transfer Techniques and Tax Minimization

Beyond business continuity, advanced wealth transfer strategies offer families the ability to minimize taxation, maximize growth, and ensure that wealth is preserved across generations. These techniques, while complex, demonstrate the sophistication of modern estate planning, blending legal ingenuity with financial acumen. Among the most powerful are Grantor Retained Annuity Trusts (GRATs), sales to Intentionally Defective Grantor Trusts (IDGTs), and Qualified Personal Residence Trusts (QPRTs). Each leverages statutory frameworks to transfer value efficiently, reduce estate inclusion, and secure tax advantages while maintaining alignment with family goals.

GRATs exemplify the principle of leveraging time and valuation. By transferring appreciating assets into a GRAT, the grantor retains an annuity stream for a fixed term, with the remainder passing to heirs if the assets outperform a specified rate set by the IRS. The beauty of GRATs lies in their asymmetry: if the assets underperform, the grantor has simply received back what was contributed, but if they exceed expectations, the excess growth escapes estate taxation. Asset selection is therefore critical. Highly volatile or appreciating assets—such as shares in growing companies—can deliver outsized benefits. Timing of valuation further enhances outcomes, as funding GRATs during market downturns locks in lower starting values, amplifying subsequent appreciation.

Rolling GRATs extend this strategy, with grantors establishing consecutive short-term GRATs to continually transfer appreciation. Each new GRAT captures incremental growth, compounding benefits across time. Term optimization is equally important, as shorter terms reduce mortality risk but may limit growth capture, while longer terms increase the chance of estate inclusion if the grantor dies during the term. Families often combine GRATs with Charitable Lead Annuity Trusts (CLATs), blending tax minimization with philanthropy. CLATs allow for charitable lead payments while ultimately transferring remainder interests to heirs, integrating giving with transfer efficiency.

Sales to Intentionally Defective Grantor Trusts (IDGTs) represent another cornerstone strategy. Here, the grantor sells appreciating assets to a trust in exchange for a promissory note, structured with interest at IRS-approved rates. Because the trust is intentionally defective for income tax purposes, the sale does not trigger capital gains, and the grantor continues to pay income taxes on trust earnings. This arrangement functions as an additional, tax-free transfer of wealth, as the grantor's tax payments reduce their estate without constituting taxable gifts. Over time, appreciation in excess of the note's interest accrues to the trust, outside the estate. Note forgiveness strategies may further reduce estate inclusion, though they require careful compliance to avoid triggering gift tax.

QPRTs offer a specialized vehicle for transferring residences while minimizing estate impact. By placing a primary or vacation residence into a QPRT, the grantor retains the right to live in the property for a fixed term, after which ownership passes to beneficiaries. The value of the gift is discounted to reflect the grantor's retained interest, often reducing taxable transfers significantly. If the grantor survives the term, the residence passes outside the estate; if not, it is included, creating some risk.

Term selection becomes critical, balancing the benefits of longer terms with the mortality risk of estate inclusion. Post-term planning addresses how the grantor may continue living in the residence, often through rental agreements with beneficiaries, which further reduce the taxable estate by transferring funds without gift implications.

Illiquid assets such as residences require special attention to management and valuation. Trustees must ensure that properties are maintained, insured, and transferred in accordance with trust terms. Vacation properties often carry emotional value, and QPRTs provide a structured framework for preserving family traditions while also achieving tax efficiency. When combined with dynasty trust structures, QPRTs ensure that residences remain available for multiple generations, anchoring legacy not only in financial assets but also in places of shared memory.

These advanced techniques illustrate the layered sophistication of modern estate planning. GRATs exploit growth beyond statutory assumptions, IDGTs convert tax payments into silent wealth transfers, and QPRTs transform residences into instruments of legacy. Each requires careful timing, valuation, and structuring, but together they empower families to achieve outcomes far beyond what basic planning can offer.

What unites them is not technical novelty but purpose: the preservation and transfer of wealth in ways that maximize opportunity for heirs while minimizing erosion from taxes. By integrating these strategies, families achieve the efficiencies that studies confirm—transferring 25 to 35 percent more wealth compared to basic wills—while also embedding structures that reflect values, resilience, and foresight. In doing so, they reaffirm

Benjamin Franklin's maxim, demonstrating that investment in knowledge, when applied through careful planning, yields dividends measured not only in dollars but in the endurance of legacy.

Conclusion: Building Your Legacy Through Strategic Trust Planning

The landscape of trust planning is not static. It is a living system, one that shifts in response to technological innovation, legislative reform, and the evolving realities of family life. What was once a discipline centered largely on wills, land, and probate avoidance has become a sophisticated arena where digital wealth, cross-border holdings, and multi-generational governance all converge. Families today face a world of unprecedented complexity, but also of unprecedented opportunity. Strategic trust planning has emerged not only as a way to preserve financial capital but also as a way to protect values, guide future generations, and secure a legacy that endures beyond the limits of a single lifetime.

The future of trust planning lies in adaptability. Tax laws change with political winds, interest rates rise and fall, and market cycles challenge even the most carefully designed portfolios. Families themselves evolve as children marry, businesses expand, or heirs settle in different parts of the globe. A rigid trust structure may falter under these pressures, but modern trusts, built with flexibility and foresight, can thrive. The integration of trust protectors, decanting provisions, and distribution committees allows documents to breathe, to evolve without losing their essence. Similarly, the recognition of digital assets as part of estate planning ensures that cryptocurrency wallets, domain names, and online businesses receive the same careful stewardship once reserved for farms, factories, and brokerage accounts. International considerations have become equally vital, as global wealth demands compliance with reporting regimes, coordination of treaties, and governance structures that bridge cultures and legal systems. Families who embrace these innovations are not simply responding to change; they are preparing their legacies to flourish in a world defined by change.

Success in trust planning is rarely the product of isolated effort. The most effective structures arise from collaboration between professionals and family members alike. Attorneys bring knowledge of statutes and fiduciary frameworks, accountants navigate the intricacies of valuation and taxation, and investment advisors craft strategies that preserve and grow wealth over decades. Yet these technical skills alone are insufficient if families fail to communicate. Trust disputes rarely begin with numbers; they begin with silence, misunderstanding, and the absence of shared vision. Families who incorporate regular meetings, transparent reporting, and clearly articulated mission statements into their planning cultivate more than efficiency. They cultivate cohesion, teaching heirs that wealth is not merely inherited but entrusted. When families understand the principles underlying their trusts, they are less likely to perceive distributions as arbitrary or unfair and more likely to embrace their role as stewards of a shared legacy.

Flexibility must always be balanced with efficiency. A trust that adapts too easily risks losing direction, while one that is overly rigid may crack under pressure. The most successful trusts strike equilibrium. They preserve the grantor's intent while allowing for adjustments that reflect changing law and circumstance. They offer tax efficiency without neglecting the human dimension of care and guidance. They empower trustees with discretion but frame that discretion within values that echo across generations.

In doing so, they achieve something that neither purely financial planning nor purely legal drafting can deliver: a structure that embodies both the technical and the moral dimensions of legacy.

Taking action is the essential next step. Knowledge, no matter how comprehensive, achieves nothing without implementation. The first task is an honest assessment of your current estate planning situation. Do your existing documents reflect your present wealth, family structure, and objectives? Have you accounted for digital assets, international holdings, or changes in tax law? Are your heirs prepared, both financially and emotionally, to assume the responsibilities of stewardship? These questions are not academic; they are practical, and the answers determine whether your legacy will be preserved or dissipated.

Professional guidance is indispensable in navigating these questions. Modern trust planning requires not only technical expertise but also interdisciplinary coordination. A skilled attorney may craft provisions that allow for modification, but without the input of a financial advisor who understands long-term investment horizons, those provisions may lack practical strength. An accountant may design tax-efficient funding strategies, but without clear communication to beneficiaries, those strategies may foster resentment rather than gratitude. A comprehensive team ensures that no element is neglected, and that each component reinforces the others in service of your broader objectives.

Family engagement is equally crucial. A trust, however well-designed, cannot succeed if beneficiaries view it as a mysterious or controlling instrument. Families who engage heirs early—educating them in financial literacy, involving them in philanthropic initiatives, or inviting them into advisory roles—prepare them not only to receive wealth but to carry it forward responsibly. Governance structures such as family constitutions or advisory councils formalize these efforts, embedding values and expectations into the very culture of the family. In this way, wealth ceases to be a source of conflict and becomes a medium for connection.

The journey of trust planning is not linear, nor is it ever complete. Laws will continue to evolve, markets will fluctuate, and families will grow in unexpected ways. A trust created today may serve for a century or more, but only if it is designed to adapt without losing its core. Regular reviews, ongoing professional engagement, and open dialogue with family ensure that your planning remains relevant. Each revision is not a failure of foresight but a demonstration of resilience, proof that your legacy is strong enough to endure change.

What this guide has sought to illustrate is that trust planning is more than a set of legal documents. It is a philosophy of stewardship, an approach to wealth that recognizes its dual nature as both opportunity and responsibility. By integrating strategies for tax minimization, asset protection, business succession, philanthropy, and digital wealth, families construct legacies that transcend individual lifespans. By embedding communication, education, and shared values into their governance, they ensure that wealth serves as a unifying force rather than a divisive one.

Your next steps are clear: assess, engage, implement, and refine. Begin with a comprehensive review of your current position, identify the gaps and vulnerabilities, and consult professionals who can guide you with both technical precision and a vision for continuity. Involve your family not as passive recipients but as active participants, shaping a shared future that reflects your values. Build flexibility into your structures, but never lose sight of the principles you wish to preserve.

Legacy is not built in a single act but through deliberate steps, taken consistently over time. Each decision you make in structuring a trust, each conversation you hold with heirs, each adjustment you pursue in response to new laws or new technologies—these are the bricks and mortar of a legacy that can endure. In preparing thoughtfully, you ensure that your wealth not only sustains but uplifts, not only transfers but transforms.

The journey does not end with the signing of documents or the funding of a trust. It is an ongoing process of adaptation, refinement, and reaffirmation of values. By embracing the principles and strategies explored throughout this guide, you are positioned to navigate complexity with confidence and to turn wealth into an enduring gift. In doing so, you fulfill the essence of strategic trust planning: the creation of a legacy that serves not just as a record of what you built, but as a foundation upon which generations to come may continue to build.